ACHIEVE MANUFACTURING EXCELLENCE LEAN AND SMART MANUFACTURING

REQUIREMENT FOR THE SUCCESSFUL IMPLEMENTATION OF THE FACTORY OF THE FUTURE

DR AZLAN NITHIA

PARTRIDGE

Copyright © 2019 by Dr Azlan Nithia.

Library of Congress Control Number: 2019906796
ISBN: Hardcover 978-1-5437-5177-2
Softcover 978-1-5437-5178-9
eBook 978-1-5437-5179-6

All rights reserved. No part of this book may be used or reproduced by any means, graphic, electronic, or mechanical, including photocopying, recording, taping or by any information storage retrieval system without the written permission of the author except in the case of brief quotations embodied in critical articles and reviews.

Because of the dynamic nature of the Internet, any web addresses or links contained in this book may have changed since publication and may no longer be valid. The views expressed in this work are solely those of the author and do not necessarily reflect the views of the publisher, and the publisher hereby disclaims any responsibility for them.

Print information available on the last page.

To order additional copies of this book, contact
Toll Free 800 101 2657 (Singapore)
Toll Free 1 800 81 7340 (Malaysia)
orders.singapore@partridgepublishing.com

www.partridgepublishing.com/singapore

Contents

Acknowledgements vii
Preface ix
Introduction xi

Chapter 1
Leadership and Competitiveness 1
- Senior Leaders' Commitment 1
- Three Drivers of Manufacturing Competitiveness 4

Chapter 2
Eliminating the 3M Wastes 10
- The 3M Wastes in Manufacturing 10
- MUDA (Waste) 11
- Mura (Unevenness) 15
- Case Study: Overcoming Constraints in the
  Production System 18
- Muri (Overburdened) 21
- Andon System 23
- Value Stream Mapping (VSM) 24

Chapter 3
The Journey for Continuous Improvement 30
- Early Detection and Immediate Action 30

Chapter 4
Organisation and People Culture 40
- Manufacturing Excellence 3M House 40
- People Culture Is the Foundation 42

Chapter 5
Smart Manufacturing: Factory of the Future 68
- The Inevitable Manufacturing Transition................................. 68
- Steps to Become Factory of the Future 70
- Transitioning to Factory of the Future 74
- Smart Manufacturing and Market Competitiveness 75
- The Industrial Revolution 78

Conclusion 85

Appendix 1
- Kaizen Event to Deliver Breakthrough Results 89
- Key Thoughts on Lean (The Lean Enterprise) 96
- Intimate Customer Knowledge to Grow the Business 98
- Problem-Solving Case Study:
  A Case of the Porous Castings 101
- Inspiring Learning to Develop Talent Requirement
  for Smart Manufacturing Implementation 121

References...137

Acknowledgements

My first book was published in 2018 and was titled *Transitioning into New Manufacturing Paradigm: To Succeed in the Customer-Centric Business Environment—Agility, Speed and Responsiveness* 'The Lean Manufacturing Enterprise'.

My second book further expanded the lean manufacturing concepts and is important as the foundation for the readiness and implementation of smart manufacturing to achieve the status of the factory of the future.

In the course of writing both my books, I have benefitted from the experiences of many experts and academics, both locally and abroad. I must admit that I cannot take all the credit expressed in this book because I have merely brought together my vast years of experiences from high-volume manufacturing, one-piece production, digital product development, lean implementations, digital connectivity, automation, robotics, and lessons from many experienced gurus and sensei from the various industries around the world.

My early adoption of lean principles began when I first read the book *The Machine That Changed the World* by James Womack (who introduced lean to the world), the book *Kaizen: The Key to Japan's Competitive Success* by Masaaki Imai (who introduced kaizen to world), and the book *Toyota Production System: Beyond Large-Scale Production* by Taiichi Ohno (who founded and introduced the Toyota production system or TPS). These books started my relentless search for manufacturing excellence, and this search led me to numerous types of research into various manufacturing systems, TPS, lean practices, and the influence of organisational culture.

Later, I was privileged to meet and learn more from a person who had worked directly with Mr Maasaki Imai; and he wrote his own book, *Chronicles of a Quality Detective* by Dr Shrinivas Gondhalekar (aka Dr G). Dr G introduced to the world one of the most powerful approaches towards solving quality problems by using a simple methodology called differential diagnosis (DD). I had personally worked with Dr G for more than fifteen years, solving hundreds of quality problems and implementing numerous lean and kaizen activities successfully.

I like to thank Professor Dr Gondhalekar for his kindness for contributing his amazing expertise in solving the unsolvable problem case study in this book as written in 'Appendix 4: Problem-Solving Case Study: A Case of the Porous Castings'.

My thanks to Major Dr J. Prebagaran for his kindness for contributing in this book as written in 'Appendix 5: Inspiring Learning to Develop Talent Requirement for Smart Manufacturing Implementation'.

Preface

Over the years, I have worked with many manufacturing organisations around the world, particularly those engaged in high-volume mass manufacturing. I have spent more than thirty-five years in various manufacturing functions, product development, and automated high-volume tooling manufacturing operations and successfully transformed several manufacturing organisations.

The customers prefer small-lot sizes, multiple models (model variations), short delivery lead times, and low cost. If the organisation cannot transition quickly to the new manufacturing paradigm of buyer-centric strategy and rapidly changing customer demands, the rigidity of the manufacturing industries and the inability to transform will eliminate them from the industry. This problem was further complicated when these organisations embarked into capital-intensive automation journey to reduce labour cost by implementing robots and high-technology machines; this increased the rigidity, lengthened the product changeover time, and further complicated and stiffened the internal processes.

The manufacturing sector has seen major evolution since the first Industrial Revolution and throughout the challenging fourth Industrial Revolution that introduced high levels of digital connectivity and sophisticated automated human-machine interfaces. The manufacturing industry is constantly evolving from the use of intensive labour force to the use of automation and robotics to increase production efficiency and reduce the cost of labour.

These advanced technological applications require a strong lean manufacturing foundation and readiness prior to implementing the smart manufacturing, which requires advanced technology processes.

An efficient manufacturing organisation must pave the way to enhance the company's customer responsiveness, increase productivity, reduce lead time, reduce labour dependency, and reduce product cost.

I strongly believe the transition into lean and smart manufacturing paradigm is important for the survival of any manufacturing organisation to achieve manufacturing excellence and compete successfully with the customer-centric strategy.

In the end, all industries will remain as business but as a smart-connected business in a digitally connected world. These smart businesses will have the innovative twist of innovation and transformational digital technologies of business models and processes that will increase profit, decrease product costs, enhance the consumer experience, optimise consumer loyalty through lifetime value, and increase global market with innovative growth, but still remain relevant and responsive to any market digital disruptions.

Building the kind of management and organisational culture in which everyone can contribute directly to adding value for the customers is important. Keep the lean and kaizen spirit alive to constantly improve and strengthen the manufacturing foundation so that smart manufacturing can be efficiently implemented and able to deliver the required customer responsiveness. To become a customer-driven company, the companies must become solutions providers, looking for gaps in the supply chain and what the customers need that no one is providing. The goal of our value innovation must be to create the top-line growth and sales growth and gain the market share.

Introduction

There are many industries and businesses around the world that are embracing the concept of lean manufacturing to deliver higher levels of customer responsiveness. These organisations are embarking into a lean journey to drive lead time down, reduce inventories, take cost out, improve quality, improve throughput, reduce non-value-added activities, and focus on customer responsiveness.

The focus of the new industrial revolution is to achieve smart manufacturing and the status of factory of the future. To achieve this, it requires the successful implementation of the connected factory. This will require the machines, robots, and processes to be digitally connected to deliver real-time analysis and monitoring for performance and efficiencies.

To take advantage of these important digital technologies, the internal manufacturing processes and equipment must be operating very efficiently. They must be predictable, and processes are performing at their optimum levels. The foundations for this are lean manufacturing principles and the focus to remove the 3M wastes (*muda*, *mura*, and *muri*) from the whole manufacturing system. If non-value-added activities or poor-performing processes are not eliminated or improved, then, the connected factory concept will merely mean connecting the low-performing processes and machines, which are non-value-adding and are wastes of the company's resources and investments.

Smart manufacturing should mean the organisation is already practising lean manufacturing and is able to deliver high customer responsiveness, continuously reducing lead times. It's able to achieve mass customisation of products and is very agile, constantly lowering cost. Without meeting these few basic customer requirements, no business can ever continue to survive in today's and the future's hypercompetitive marketplace.

The internet and the IoT (internet of things) have simplified the whole value chain and made it highly responsive to meet customer needs. They shifted the real-time decision-making power to the end consumer (customer-centric and pull system). They would place orders directly in the internet; and then the manufacturing centres would respond to the orders in a real-time basis, already eliminating most of the intermediaries. This also means the manufacturing process centres (or the manufacturing companies) must be connected and respond to customers' orders quickly. They must be able to produce small orders and in various models at low cost and with efficiency. In the connected IoT environment, it is extremely critical to ensure the manufacturing organisations are constantly performing at their optimum, and the weakest manufacturers who cannot meet these requirements will get eliminated.

The lean manufacturing is not another cost-reduction exercise but an important organisational strategy to relentlessly drive towards manufacturing excellence; it is a journey towards achieving operational perfection. I have seen many companies that had embarked into lean to reduce cost or to reduce people as their only objective. This is a dangerous and wrong approach to lean journey. Lean is about developing a new organisational culture that engages everyone in the organisation into creating a relentless journey to operationalise the continuous improvement and learning culture, and it must be practised like the company's DNA at all levels of the organisation, and it requires to be nourished as a daily work culture in the company.

The successful organisations that are engaged in the lean journey will achieve breakthrough results. These breakthrough results are achieved because of the passionate support, focus, and commitment from their senior leadership, including the president and the CEO of the organisation. The lean implementation must be driven from top down (it is leadership driven), and the execution and implementation must be done at all levels. The lean is not implemented in a section or in one function; but it is an organisation-wide programme, with end-to-end system focus, whereby everyone is engaged and involved to deliver improvements constantly.

The word *kaizen* is widely used in many different industries (including hospitals, banks, hotels, and various other service industries) and organisations around the world, especially those in the journey to embrace lean principles as a company culture.

In 1986, Masaaki Imai introduced the principles of kaizen to the world in his book titled *Kaizen: The Key to Japan's Competitive Success* followed by another book titled *Gemba Kaizen: A Commonsense, Low-Cost Approach to Management* in 2001.

It roots back to a Japanese industrial engineer named Taiichi Ohno who is considered to be the father or the founder of TPS. It was later known as lean manufacturing in the United States and outside Japan. Ohno devised the concept of the seven wastes (or called the *muda* in Japanese) as part of this TPS. He wrote several books including *Toyota Production System: Beyond Large-Scale Production* (English translation in 1988).

Shigeo Shingo, who had worked with Ohno, published the book *The Study on Toyota Production System* in 1981 and later the English translation in 1989. He, together with Ohno, invented the just-in-time system, which is the backbone of TPS.

Jeffrey K. Liker, in later days, wrote the book called *The Toyota Way: 14 Management Principles from World's Greatest Manufacturer* in 2004.

The TPS consists of two key principles:

- continuous improvement
- respect for people

It also has an explicit focus to always meet the *end customer's expectation*.

The lean concepts and principles started becoming very popular amongst the industries outside Japan especially since 2000. The term *lean* was first introduced by Jim Womack in his book titled *The Machine that Changed the World* in 1990; and in this book. Lean manufacturing encompasses the benefits associated with both mass production and customised small-lot-size production while avoiding high cost by using highly flexible and modular systems, machines, and agile workforce to produce different varieties of products in low volumes with low-cost efficiently. Lean manufacturers set their sights explicitly on the end customer, embark in a journey towards perfection, continuously remove waste, continually reduce product cost, increase product variety, and always satisfy the customer's changing needs.

I have met many industry leaders who have embarked into the journey of implementing lean and driving continuous-improvement culture in their respective organisations. One of the critical gaps I find consistently in many organisations is the lack of the understanding and the importance of eliminating the 3M wastes in their manufacturing operations. Many organisations are pursuing lean and continuous-improvement programmes, but they do not understand the criticalness of eliminating or reducing the 3M wastes in their organisations.

The organisations that are in the lean journey are constantly proving that there is always a better way. This creates the culture of 'every day a better way', which is the core of the continuous-improvement culture. The best method to discover the rhythm and the flow of any factory or organisation is to understand the flow through the whole system. They start from the supplier delivering the raw material and follow the whole flow of the material through the various processes until the final assembly, packing, shipping, and loading into the container. This will merely complete the internal flow, but this is not enough to understand the whole scope of lean supply chain. The end of the flow is when the customer receives the product (or when the payment is received). Therefore, the flow starts from receiving the raw material (the ordering lead time must be included), and the end is the time when the customer receives the product.

This book is intended to provide practical approaches to enhance the effectiveness of lean manufacturing implementation by focusing on the key components of lean strategy—that is, eliminating the 3M wastes, continuous improvement, and people culture. The relentless journey to eliminate those 3M wastes (the enemies of lean) will enable the organisation to achieve manufacturing excellence. The continuous and relentless effort to remove the 3M wastes is one of the key components of TPS. The respect for people is equally important as well. Any form of waste that exists in the manufacturing system or the administrative processes is classified as non-value-adding; and it directly deters or impedes the initiatives to achieve lead-time reduction, throughput improvement, cost reduction, on-time deliveries, and quality improvements. The ultimate focus of lean is to continuously reduce the lead time and to improve the flow and rapid respond to changing customer's needs. To achieve this objective, eliminating the 3M wastes is important. Equally important in the lean journey is to implement the processes that are agile and flexible (example multi-model production, modular production line, and quick changeovers) to meet the changing customer requirements for model variations and small-lot production needs. The outcome of the lean journey will be constantly reducing delivery lead times and cost, which will obviously improve the organisation's competitive edge in the industry.

The customers are constantly demanding more rapid changes all the time. If you don't improve or adapt your organisation's culture to those changing demands, then you will never meet customer's expectation. All these requirements are the key foundations and the important operational readiness required to implement the digitally connected factory to achieve the status of the factory of the future.

List of Figures

Figure 1: Lead-Time Reduction 7
Figure 2: Product Cost Reduction 8
Figure 3: Weekly Scheduling—Unevenness (Mura Waste) 17
Figure 4: Before and After Reducing the Mura Waste 20
Figure 5: Mura Actual Case Study 21
Figure 6: Value Stream Mapping (VSM) 27
Figure 7: Sustainable Continuous Improvement—the Journey 38
Figure 8: Manufacturing Excellence—3M House 42
Figure 9: Focus on Why Parts Are Good 49
Figure 10: PVC Part Load, Punch, and Cap Assembly Machine 50
Figure 11: The Gap Equals to Problem 51
Figure 12: The Five-Step Problem-Solving Approach 55
Figure 13: Visual Performance Management.. 58
Figure 14: Job Function Involvement Model 66
Figure 15: Steps to Become Factory of the Future (AURI Model) 71
Figure 16: Lean and Smart Manufacturing—Transitioning to Factory of the Future 74
Figure 17: Smart Manufacturing Implementation versus Market Competitiveness 76

List of Tables

Table 1: Categories of Competencies 128
Table 2: Competency Dictionary 129
Table 3: Malcolm Knowles's Five Assumptions of Adult Learners 132

CHAPTER 1

Leadership and Competitiveness

Senior Leaders' Commitment

To begin the lean journey and to create a lean culture is hard. It needs the organisation's leadership team's commitment for a long-run, long-term perspective. It is an ongoing journey without no finish line or an end date. It is better not to start this journey if the senior leaders and the management team are not willing to begin and stay on this difficult but important journey. This journey is part of a larger movement, which is the enabler for manufacturing excellence required to establish the strong foundations for smart manufacturing, meet the requirements for the factory of the future, and achieve the vision of a connected factory. This must be achieved with increased customer responsiveness, low cost, and mass customisation (small-lot sizes, mix-model production, quick response, and increased degree of product variety). New organisational work cultures are not created in a few months; it will take years with passionate commitment to operationalise a seamless new work culture until it becomes the company's DNA. This requires a genuine senior leadership involvement, and this is the key to the success of this lean journey. Without it, the effort is limited, and the operations team will be powerless.

The top leaders must be committed to build the kind of management in which everyone could contribute directly to adding value for customers and taking responsibility for leading the culture change. Failing to see this as a major required cultural change and assigning the programme to middle managers to deploy is a major mistake. To live a business transformation that puts customers first and doing it by developing its people have to start from the top leader's commitment. Lean is not only about removing waste, even though this is a key component. Lean is about creating a new culture and living it.

The leadership cannot deploy lean structure and call it a lean office, employ continuous-improvement officers, and assign them to apply lean in every area of the organisation. But the management continues to do what it used to do, not being fully involved and not passionately interested. Then, the management team gets surprised that after gathering all the low-hanging, easy-to-do improvements, the whole lean sinks in the water. Later, the lean effort is abandoned; and the management looks for the next programme of the year to embark on. The lean journey and creation of a culture of continuous improvement is not a toolkit or a roadmap. Everyone in the organisation, top down, must understand it and live it so it continuously evolves.

It will negatively impact the value creation in an organization if the senior leaders (especially CEOs and CFOs) views manufacturing division as a division that derails the focus of managing the business, very capital intensive, handling people issues in manufacturing division is difficult, it is dirty and a difficult job. They rather have some other company to do the manufacturing portion. This view is a clear indication of the senior leadership lacking the understanding and knowledge of how and where the product value is created. The value is created when the organisation has total control of the supply chain, total lead time, quality, cost, and customer responsiveness.

In my opinion, organisations that already have their own brands (or IPs) already have their in-house manufacturing, product design and development capabilities, and own marketing and sales team must seriously commit and stay on the lean journey because they have the total control of the supply chain (end to end); and the manufacturing function is an excellent value creator to the business, for both upstream and downstream. Some of these examples are companies like the car companies (Honda, Toyota, Mercedes, Nissan, Ford, etc.), Lego, Samsung, Robert Borsch, B. Braun, Nestle, and many more successful companies. These are the organisations that have total end-to-end control, from product creation to product development, all the way up to delivering the products to the consumers and the cost the consumers are willing to pay. They have total control of the supply chain with the ability to continuously improve the performance by designing product for lean manufacturing, total lead-time reduction, inventory control, quality, and total cost and continuously improving the customer responsiveness.

There are also certain organisations that already have the total control of the end-to-end supply chain with in-house capabilities for product design (own brands), manufacturing, marketing, and sales. Sadly, some of these organisations may encounter strategic changes from the new senior leadership: CEO and CFO who are in the top leadership position with a very different perspective about their current manufacturing operations. They may have no manufacturing experience and the understanding of how manufacturing division creates value and constantly adds value for the business. Instead, they view manufacturing as a difficult burden to manage. It is very capital intensive and bad for their cash flow. In this case, the organisation changes its strategy; it rather buy versus make it in-house (manufacturing). These are the senior leaders who do not understand the power of lean strategy or lean manufacturing and how manufacturing plays a key role to improve customer responsiveness, reduce lead time, and improve cost. This kind of poor short-term-thinking leadership perspectives will derail the organisation's end-to-end future capabilities, especially when these senior leaders make decisions to shut down their existing manufacturing divisions.

Take control of the total end-to-end supply chain to deliver products at shorter lead time and lower cost. This allows the organisation to implement the design for lean manufacturing to achieve high manufacturing productivity and efficiencies. This delivers to the organisation a huge advantage and opportunity to achieve the best cost and lead time. If the organisation outsources manufacturing, buying instead of making, it will be very difficult for the organisation to move forward with the initiatives to continuously improve or reduce lead time and cost. It will become dependent on the outsourced vendor's manufacturing strategies, capabilities, and manufacturing systems limitations.

To successfully begin this lean journey, it will solely dependent on the senior leaders' commitment to embark on this difficult but important journey to create a strong foundation. Lean is about developing the kaizen spirit (continuous improvement and continuous learning) in every employee.

Three Drivers of Manufacturing Competitiveness

To achieve the manufacturing excellence, it is a journey. It is a journey pursued by the organisation's leaders and employees by actively engaging and cultivating the culture of continuous improvement. The dedicated focus must be to improve the three-important high-level performance drivers of organisational competitiveness in the marketplace to achieve manufacturing excellence.

The three manufacturing excellence drivers are the following:

1. Lead-Time Reduction

Continuously reduce the total end-to-end supply chain lead time and model changeover time, focus on agility, and eliminate the process rigidity. Always meet the customer delivery commitments of on-time-in-full deliveries (OTIF). There are many components of activities and events in the manufacturing systems that contribute towards the lead time. Examples could be repeated product design changes, rework, waiting for decision, suppliers' lead time, and many more.

Lead time is a key driver of competitive advantage at the marketplace and critical for the customers. It is also a key driver of cost in the organisation; therefore, to reduce lead time means to reduce or eliminate all the obstacles in the flow of the products and information. Lead-time reduction is not a one-time event; it is an event that must be carried out constantly, year on year. The method used to establish the current lead time is by doing the VSM (value stream mapping). From the VSM kaizen, the VA (value-added) and NVA (non-value-added) work and activities can be identified. The NVA must be the key focus. Constantly, the company must embark in the journey of reducing the NVA, which also means reducing the constraints and obstacles to the flow. By reducing the obstacles to the flow, the flow increases; the increase in process and product flow will reduce the lead time and increase throughput. It can be equated to a river. When there are many rocks and blockages in the river, the flow of water in the river is not smooth and the water flow frequently get obstructed. When all those rocks and blockages are removed, the river flows very smoothly; and we can see a smooth flow of water in the river without any turbulence. The same applies to any manufacturing operation in any industry.

The organisation must complete a VSM kaizen every year and constantly keep identifying and removing the NVA from the system, and the actions required to reduce the NVA can be accomplished in a kaizen event. The VSM activity will be covered in the later chapters. To reduce or eliminate inventories (inventories are also considered as obstruction to flow) and the work in process (WIP) is one of the key objectives of the VSM kaizen. The inventories are the obstacles to the flow (like rocks in the river), and they reduce the speed of flow; therefore, the reduction of it will speed up the flow and increase the lead time. It is very important to understand the concept flow in manufacturing. The best flow is achieved only when there are no obstacles to flow. The muda, mura, and muri—all of these 3M wastes—create obstacle to flow. By reducing all these obstacles, then, the flow will increase, the lead time will reduce, and the throughput will increase. When the lead time is reduced, this will obviously pave the way for more available time for production; therefore, the throughput will increase.

2. Product Cost Reduction

The organisation must continuously reduce the total cost of the product and the cost of services for the customers, year on year. Always focus efforts to reduce and eliminate the 3M wastes in the system; all of them impact the cost negatively. Constantly strive to reduce them and reduce the product cost. For this year, the concept on cost must be lower than last year without scarifying any quality and customer delight.

There are numerous economic elements that will impact the product cost. Examples are the material cost increases, salary increases, and other services related cost increases. The organisation must always strive to mitigate all these cost increases by focusing on various cost-reducing programmes, especially the 3M wastes. The organisation must never attempt to pass the cost increases to the customers because, in the long run, there will be other competitors who will be able to deliver better cost and lead time than yours. If, internally, the organisations are always focused on reducing the operational and material cost and improving quality, then, mitigating any cost increases becomes very possible. The organisations that do not focus on year-on-year product cost reduction will soon find themselves getting eliminated from the marketing competition.

3. Improvement of Throughput

The throughput, in most cases, will increase if the lead time is reduced. To continuously improve the production throughput means producing the output with good-quality products (meet customer expectations), meeting all the customer requirements, and always meeting the customer delivery expectations (on time, in full). These are all important. The process engineers and supervisors must understand the lean flow, as well as constraints and bottlenecks in the flow. The deployment of 3M wastes is critical. Constantly finding for the mura and muri in the system smoothens out the constraints and the flow obstacles. It is a relentless effort to continuously focus on finding, reducing, and eliminating constraints in the system. It is common to keep finding new constraints after the earlier constraints were eliminated. It is an ongoing journey working towards achieving perfection in manufacturing flow.

Below are two charts that show the lead-time reduction (new product launch) and product cost reduction. Both are based on an actual case study (done over ten years) and the achievement of an organisation that was very focused to relentlessly reduce the lead time, increase throughput, and decrease the cost, year after year.

After ten years of continuously improving (reducing) the lead time and product cost, the results of business competitiveness are obvious. The lead time was reduced from 40 weeks to only 15 weeks (270% reduction), and the product cost was reduced from $4.50 per item to only $1.90 per item (230% reduction). With the constant reduction of lead time (relentlessly reducing the 3M wastes and improving the flow), the total throughput of the company was increased from 5 million units a year to 30 million units a year—a sixfold throughput increase with fewer resources. This was achieved even with the constant rising of cost pressures, increased customer expectations and complexity, increased material cost, and yearly salary increases.

Figure 1: Lead-Time Reduction

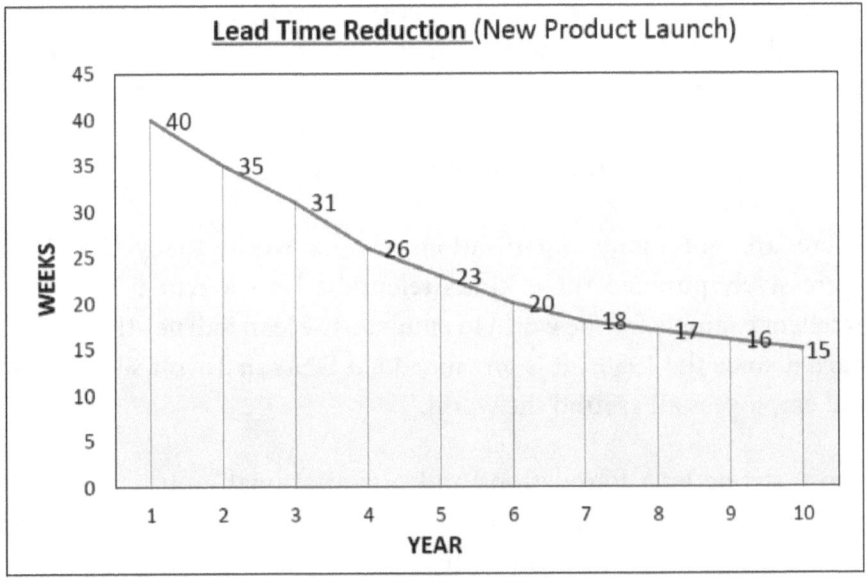

Source: Azlan Nithia, 2019

Figure 2: Product Cost Reduction

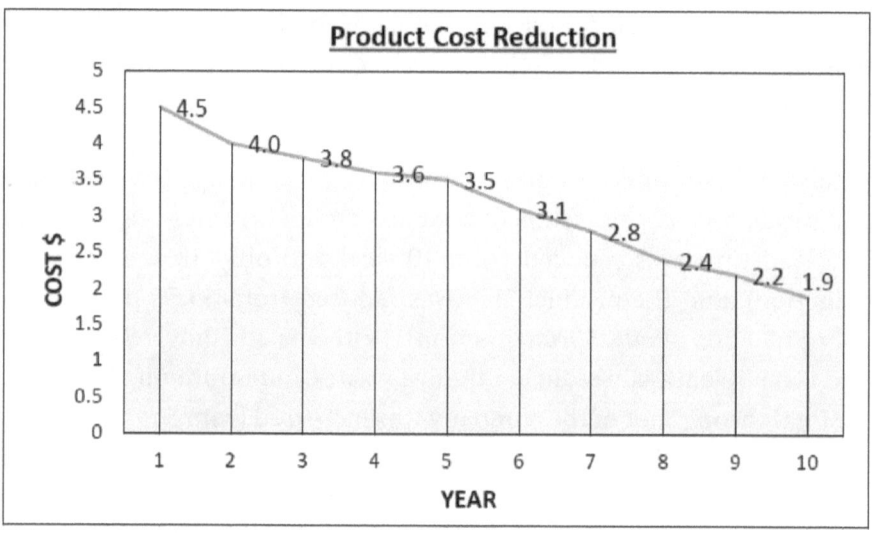

Source: Azlan Nithia, 2019

This company is now well positioned to compete in its business, eliminate its competitors, and be a global leader in the industry. It is about competing against their own performance. The people were never satisfied with the current performance. This is the lean spirit of driving continuous-improvement culture and living it daily. Currently, this company is extremely competitive in cost, quality, and lead time; it is almost impossible to find another company to beat them.

There are not many organisations in the world today that have aggressively pursued these kinds relentless lean journey. TPS is an excellent example for the world to emulate, the lean journey that Toyota started since the 1950s. It is an embedded DNA in Toyota's leadership and employees all around the world.

Those strong lean foundations and organisational culture that were implemented and operationalised in the above company have developed an efficient, smart ecosystem in this company to implement the smart-connected factory of the future. After completing the implementation of connected factory and the IoT projects, this company has further improved it customer responsiveness and further reduced lead time and cost while improving its product quality.

The continuous improvements in lead time, product cost, and throughput must be compounded with good quality and OTIF delivery. The quality and delivery commitments are the basic requirements for any organisation to stay in business. An organisation cannot survive in any business or industry by delivering bad-quality products or bad services or by missing the delivery commitments to its customers.

A good sustainable product (or service) quality, on-time delivery, and competitive cost are the core requirements for any business to survive; these apply to all types of industries. To gain and maintain the competitive advantage, the company should offer short lead time, low cost, and reliable delivery commitments (on time and in full). It should live the continuous-improvement business culture.

Only with this strong lean foundation operationalised as the company culture can the company efficiently pursue to implement the smart manufacturing, the connected factory, and the factory of the future implementation. Therefore, only by having a strong lean manufacturing foundation and then implementing smart manufacturing can the company experience improved operational efficiencies. The factory of the future will then be able to deliver better customer responsiveness, reduced lead time, and lower cost. By directly implementing smart manufacturing without a strong lean foundational culture, it can be disastrous for the operations.

Linking poor-performing machines with IoT to a centralised monitoring system will not give better output or will not improve the performance of the machines. The foundation is to have a good-performing machine. This is step one. There should also be predictable and capable machines to consistently deliver good parts. Then connecting these machines with IoT and to the centralised decision system will deliver good value for the investment (ROI), improve responsiveness and quality, and reduce cost.

CHAPTER 2

Eliminating the 3M Wastes

The 3M Wastes in Manufacturing

The 3M wastes are very often overlooked by most organisations. They exist in every organisation and industry. There are three different types of wastes in any organisation or industry. Most organisations embarking in the lean journey focus only on one type of waste, which is commonly called the muda in Japanese or, simply, waste. To achieve manufacturing excellence, there are other two key drivers of waste in the manufacturing system. They are called the mura (unevenness in the system) and the muri (overworked or overburdened process or person). Omitting the mura and muri is a big mistake in any manufacturing operation or industry because most of the wastes (muda) are created by mura and muri. These 3M wastes are the key focal points of TPS.

These three types of wastes called muda, mura, and muri are the 'enemies' of lean and must be reduced and ultimately eliminated to achieve the manufacturing excellence.

- **Muda (waste):** it means activity or process that does not add value to the customer; a physical waste of time, resources, material

- **Mura (unevenness):** it means waste of unevenness or inconsistency of processes and loading unevenness
- **Muri (overburdened):** it means that operators or machines are pushed through their natural limits, which leads to problems

If the organisation does not seriously embark on the relentless journey to reduce and eliminate the 3M wastes, then achieving manufacturing excellence may not be possible.

Elimination of 3M wastes = manufacturing excellence

It is important to understand how they are interrelated and influence one another. Mura creates waste (muda), and muri creates waste (muda); together, they impede manufacturing excellence.

Therefore, reducing mura, muri, and muda should be studied simultaneously in a never-ending quest to eliminate the 3M wastes that will enable manufacturing excellence. This must become the organisation's relentless journey to pursue the continuous-improvement culture, which forms one of the important pillars of TPS.

MUDA (Waste)

Muda is any work that is done by the organisation that the customer is not willing to pay for or does not add any extra value to the product. It is the obstacle to the process or production flow. This NVA work or obstacle (muda) to flow normally leads to the increase in lead time and increase in product cost and impedes the throughput performance. Muda is any activity or process (in manufacturing or business process) that does not add value to the customer. It is a physical waste of resources and a material waste. This is the activity carried out by the company, but this activity does not transform the product and the customer does not see or care.

There are eight types of wastes (muda) in manufacturing:

1. Defects

These are the products or services created with a defect but moved to the next process or the next step. These products do not meet or conform to the customer's specifications or requirements. When these defects or defective products are allowed to flow to the next process, these defects create extra work to rectify them or to rework them to make them good. This is a NVA work or activity. It interrupts the current WIP; and when these defective parts flow to the next process or steps, they also interrupt the flow and rhythm of work done.

It is important to cultivate the work culture of 'Do Not Make Defects, Do Not Send Defects, and Do Not Receive Defects' or 'Make Good Parts, Send Good Parts, and Receive Good Parts'.

2. Overproduction

It means producing more products than the customer needs at that point in time. This could also mean the products are more than what the subsequent process requires. This creates unwanted inventories. Inventories take up space, hold up cash (parts produced are money already spent), and increase the risk of order cancellation. Practise just-in-time (JIT) and deliver the right quantity of products and at the right time to the next process—nothing more and nothing less. It is important to measure OTIF performance for the internal processes. There are internal and external customers. The internal customer is the subsequent or the next process in the system, but the actual external customer is the final customer who receives the product or services and pays for the products or services.

3. Waiting

Parts waiting in the WIP in the shop floor, waiting for decision, waiting due to pending paperwork, and parts on hold due to poor quality are some of the wastes created due to waiting. Parts produced but are waiting will interrupt the flow sequence of the next process. Establish a system that triggers an immediate action. Machine breakdown and parts cannot be produced because waiting for a technician to repair it is also waiting. This waiting due to machine problem will create part shortages and delivery delays. This will affect the parts OTIF performance. Establish an andon (visual system) that triggers a technician to take immediate action. It is important to measure the waiting time and continuously focus on reducing this non-value-adding waste. As for the machine breakdown, it is recommended to measure machine or equipment breakdown frequency and mean time between breakdown.

4. Transport

It refers to all movements of products between workstations and processes involving multiple individuals. Any kind of movement is a waste; therefore, it is critical to create a part movement path or route that takes the shortest time and the least resources. There are numerous methods this can be achieved. Examples will be by integrating various processes in the system as flexible mini production lines that are linked as one system flow or bringing processes in the system as close as possible.

5. Inventories

These are the products or services that are waiting for next operation at a workstation and in the inventory holding stores or locations. Inventories that are waiting are waste. It is important that all inventories in the shop floor are accurately controlled by the kanban system, and there should be a visual kanban system. Kanban system manages inventories visually, the minimum and maximum inventories, and the timely part replenishment orders system deployed. This system will ensure the right parts with the right quantities are in the inventory. Nothing more and nothing less is available for the next process on time. Inventories are wastes; therefore, there must be a continuous effort undertaken to reduce them. Every part in the inventory must be prioritised with the FIFO system to ensure a continuous flow and an active customer requirement.

6. Motion

It's the movement of people and machines without working on the product or service. This is a non-value-adding or wasteful activity. Every movement of people in the shop floor must be reviewed critically, and you must find ways to reduce those movements. Mapping out the movement diagram of the people is important. This is also called spaghetti mapping. By mapping out the movement of the day or the shift, it is possible to find ideas to reduce those movements or even eliminate them completely. You will be surprised how many metres or even kilometres a person walks in the shop floor in a shift or a day. There are cases of employees walking up to five to six kilometres a day in a shop floor.

Similarly, it is also possible to map out the movement path of a machine or a robot. There will be numerous movements or paths taken by the machine or the robot that do not add value to the product or do not change the product form by performing those movements. By putting in a robot that makes those fanciful movements may look very interesting; but if they do not add value to the product, cut off those non-value-adding robot movements.

7. Excess Processing

It means doing extra operations on the product that the customer is not asking for or those the customer cannot see. These are wasteful activities. The quality function in the organisation must clearly understand the customer's expectation and establish quality control systems in the production processes accordingly so that the production activities are not carried out beyond the customer's expectations. There are numerous cases whereby excess work is carried out in the production by the employees on the product or in the processing due to lack of SOP (standard operating procedure) and lack of understanding of the customer expectation. SOP must be established for every process in the system, and all the employees must well trained and certified to operate the SOP effectively all the time. Any deviation from the process SOP must be reviewed very seriously, and immediate action must be taken by the process supervisor. The employees must not be allowed to deviate away from the SOPs without supervisor or management approvals. This must become an organisation culture.

8. Non-Used Talent

Employee knowledge and skills that are not being used to their fullest potential to improve the processes are regarded as wasted employee talent. As we have understood from the previous chapters, employee knowledge, involvement, and improvements are very crucial to achieve mass customisation and manufacturing excellence. Every improvement activity requires employee involvement. Optimising every employee's talent in an organisation is important to develop and achieve manufacturing excellence; and by achieving manufacturing excellence, it facilitates mass customisation process.

All the wastes or muda can be classified as 'islands of waste' in the company; therefore, there are eight islands of waste. It is important to look at the whole system and then identify all the types of waste in the whole system. The process or methodology that is effectively used in lean to systematically establish waste (NVA activities) in the whole system in an organisation is called VSM. It is important to understand the kind of waste that exists in the system by completing a VSM kaizen (start-to-end process mapping).

Mura (Unevenness)

Mura is the unevenness found in various stages of the manufacturing system, and it creates constraints and loss of system throughput.

The examples of mura or unevenness are as follows:

1. Fluctuation and changes in customer orders
2. Variations in process times and variations of cycle times for different operators

3. Failure of JIT or OTIF delivery between the processes in the system
4. Failure of processing takt time

Takt time is the cycle-time rhythm for the whole system throughput. Any process in the system not aligned to the takt time will create unevenness and lack of uniformity in the process and output. This failure will impact the flow in the system and result in mura.

If the mura is not reduced or eliminated, it increases the possibilities of overburdening (muri) of the affected underperforming process, which therefore will create muda (waste) by interrupting the flow through the system. This mura will impact lead time, output, and, obviously, product cost. Mura creates most of the eight elements of muda (waste); therefore, most often, mura creates muda and muri.

It is important to constantly identify and reduce unevenness, variations, and constraints in the production or manufacturing system by aligning all the processes.

Production Schedule Smoothening

The figure below is an example of poor production scheduling. The production scheduling method varies from one organisation to another, and the production scheduling could be planned and executed based on monthly or weekly or daily production and shipping targets.

The figure shows an example of an organisation planned on a monthly production, delivery, and shipping targets. The monthly customer's delivery target is 120,000 units of products. The normal production behaviour will be the last-week-of-the-month rush to meet the total order by the month-end cut-off date. This kind of production behaviour creates major unevenness in production processes and the system, especially in the last week of the month.

Figure 3: Weekly Scheduling—Unevenness (Mura Waste)

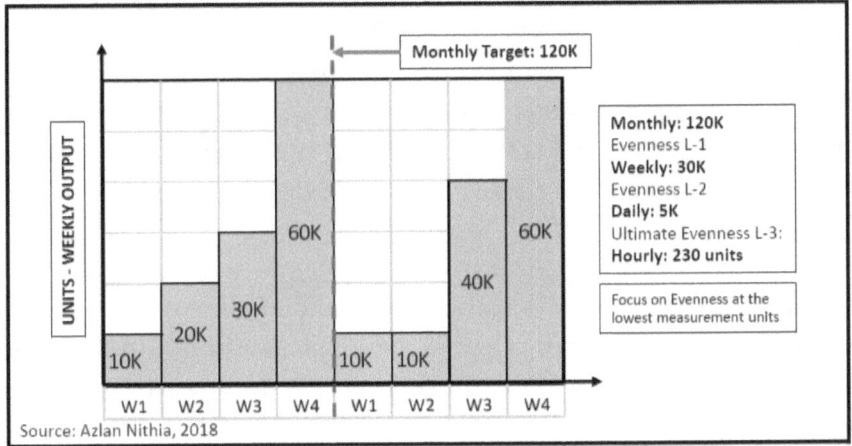

Source: Azlan Nithia, 2018

The organisations that operate on weekly scheduling targets tend to have a crazy rush to meet the targets on Friday and Saturday, again creating unevenness in between processes and various kinds of bottlenecks on the last day of the week. They also create major issues in throughput on Saturdays to meet the weekly target by Saturday night shift.

Then, what about going for daily target scheduling? Yes, it's much better than monthly and weekly scheduling system. In a daily production planning, assume the production is operating in two shift operations, morning shift and evening shift, with employees working ten hours per shift. The target cut-off will be on the second (evening) shift, on the last hour, and the twentieth hour. The target must be achieved. If this is further analysed by the hour, we will learn the major production loading would have been be on the second shift, especially the last few hours of the second shift, to meet the day's target quantity. Therefore, the constraints will be created in the last few hours of the production. Again, there's unevenness in throughput if compared from the first-hour production output and the output during the last few hours of the second shift.

The better solution to manage mura or constraints will be to schedule production targets by the hour. Every process, machine, and system is scheduled to deliver the hourly output targets. Any interruption must be resolved within the same hour (the aim is to solve problems in minutes) to ensure continuous flow of products through all the processes in the whole production system. In an hourly planning and scheduling strategy, the 120,000 units target will be broken down to hourly target of 230 units per hour (operating twenty-six days a month and twenty hours a day).

Smoothening the production scheduling to hourly is extremely critical to ensure process constraints are not developed anywhere in the whole system. Focus on operating on evenness at the lowest scheduling units. Every process and equipment must be tracked to deliver this hourly target, and every shift performance must be discussed by the production supervisor. Actions should be taken to resolve them so that these issues do not continue affecting the performance of the next or later production shift.

The front-line leaders (sometimes called line leaders) and supervisors must be actively engaged to the activities being performed at the *gemba* (workplace) so that immediate support and help can be provided to the workers having any problem with the process or machine. To facilitate this, workers calling for help or have a problem can receive assistance using andon (visual trigger for help system). Andon is triggered by pushing a button that lights up red. It has a siren or string you can pull to trigger the siren and light. The light is visual and must be easily seen from afar by the technicians and supervisors.

Case Study: Overcoming Constraints in the Production System

Let us look at the figure below (constraints in the system). This is an actual case study done on constraints in a production line. The poor throughput performance was affecting the customer order deliveries.

These constraints impacted the overall system throughput. The throughput is always constrained by the worst-performing process. The best output is constrained by the worst-limiting process. There are a total of thirty-five stations (or processes) in this production line. The cycle time of the thirty-five processes ranges from 5 to 24 seconds. The longest cycle-time processes choke the flow. In this case, it is 24 seconds (secs) in stations numbers 1, 4, 25, and 27. Even though there are processes that are running at 5 seconds, the throughput cannot be increased due to the processes operating at 24 seconds. These are the mura in the system that create unevenness in the flow and output.

The engineers did a very detailed study of every activity being done in those four limiting stations. The stations' operation sequence and activity were improved 5 to 6 seconds, reducing the mura or the constraints to the throughput. After those constraints were solved, the flow was greatly improved. Improving constraints will improve flow and increase throughput of the system. The process with the highest cycle time after improvement is 6 seconds. This translates to throughput improvement from 150 units per hour (24 seconds) to 600 units per hour (6 seconds). This translates to a 400% throughput increase.

This is the amazing power of reducing the mura and constraint. These are the initiatives the organisation must constantly be focused on to achieve excellence in their manufacturing operations. The activity of reducing the mura in the production system must be carried out as a continuous-improvement journey to achieve perfection in the flow and throughput results.

Figure 4: Before and After Reducing the Mura Waste

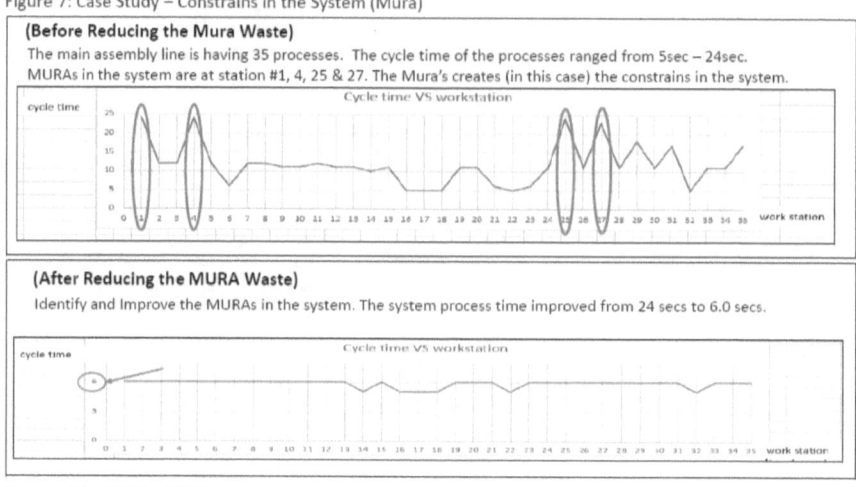

Source: Azlan Nithia, 2018

After improving the constraints as shown in the figure above, the production line can finally operate at a 6-second cycle time, which equals to 600 units per hour. This should translate to an output of 6,000 units per shift (ten-hour shifts) and 12,000 units per day (two shifts per day). But the problem was, the production supervisor was not able to deliver the 6,000 units per shift, delivering below 3,800 units per shift. That is only 63% output of the potential 6,000 units at 100%.

A team of engineers and production supervisor did the constraint study in the system, finding for the next mura or the next constraint. The team discovered the frequent production line stoppages due to shortage of part supply from another subassembly production line. The subassembly line is only delivering 380 units per hour to the main production line. The main production line is capable to produce 600 units per hour; but due to the shortages of part supply from subassembly production line, the overall system throughput was constrained at only 380 units per hour.

The team of engineers shifted the focus to improve the subassembly production line. Look at the figure 8 called subassembly processes. There are 12 subassembly processes or stations. The stations 1, 3, 5, and

12 are not able to meet the target expected at 600 units per hour. The team was able to improve the output of those four stations to produce 600 units per hour. After the constraints in the subassembly were improved to achieve the throughput of 600 units per hour, they were now able to supply the required 600 units per hour to the main production line. Finally, the total system throughput was improved and able to produce 600 units per hour.

Figure 5: Mura Actual Case Study

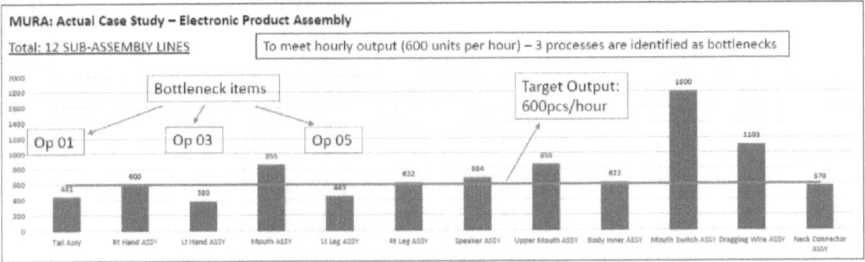

Source: Azlan Nithia, 2018

The case study demonstrated the importance to constantly find the constraints (mura) and then improve the constraints. The constraints change to a different process. As one constraint is solved, another new constraint will emerge. This is a relentless journey of continuous improvement to continuously identify and improve the system flow and improve the throughput.

Muri (Overburdened)

The third *M* is the muri. It means overburden. When a machine or person is overburdened, it can result in mura and muda wastes. Muri occurs when the workers or machines are pushed through their natural limits, which leads to many problems.

The performance of an overburdened machine or people cannot be sustained over time. The overburdened machines operating beyond their natural limits will break down. When the machine breaks down, it creates shortages of parts and impacts the target output of that process, creates unevenness of part flow to the next process, and reduces the throughput of the system. Similarly, overburdened people who work beyond their natural limits will also break down. This translates to employee absenteeism. Therefore, it is important to ensure muri is not created in the production system as well as in the administrative processes.

All machines in the production must be operated per the machine's normal operating procedures. It is a good practice to implement the OEE (overall equipment effectiveness) for all machines used in the production. It is important to maintain all machines and tools at optimum operating conditions so that unplanned breakdowns can be avoided. One method of achieving this is by establishing preventive maintenance procedure for all machines and tools used in the production processes. The production team and technicians must ensure a constant adherence to preventive maintenance (PM) procedures. Implementing autonomous maintenance is very effective to prevent unplanned breakdowns. A well-maintained machine will deliver a consistent performance.

The muri can be identified as one of an indicator of employee absenteeism, more and more people end up at home with a burnout, which means they are literally overburdened up to a point where they cannot perform (Westendorp & Van Bodegom, 2015).

Apart from absenteeism, performance as a result of the level of arousal is like a parabola in which performance increases when the arousal rises but only up to a certain point. After that, more arousal (then perceived as stress) leads to a lower performance (Yerkes & Dodson, 1908).

These are tips to help reduce people-related muri:

1. Every process and operation done must have a well-defined SOP that visually explains the job and activity of the operator at the process.
2. Team board should visually display the 5S, standard work, hours required versus available to perform the task and absenteeism.

This gives an indication of any overburdening in any production areas.
3. Production supervisors must constantly be engaged with the workers to receive feedback and listen to the problems being faced by the workers.
4. Managers must periodically have small group discussions with their employees to receive feedbacks and ideas to improve their work areas.

Not engaging the employees is a waste; it is a waste of unused employee talent. Employees must be actively involved in all the improvement programmes and encourage them to participate in daily improvement activities in their work areas.

The andon system (*jidoka*) reduces mura and muri.

To stop and fix the problems is one of the core pillars of TPS called jidoka. This action will stop more defects from being made, prevent the defective parts from flowing to the next process, and trigger the problem to be resolved immediately by the line technicians.

Andon System

The andon is the concept of jidoka, which is one of the core pillars of TPS. It is to stop and fix the problems. At Toyota, this translates into the andon, a cord hanging above the production line. Whenever an employee encounters a problem, the cord is pulled; and the production line is stopped. All employees in the line know that a problem has occurred. A visual or alarm sound system is triggered, telling them where the problem occurred. With the line being stopped, the employees can focus on immediately solving the problem. By stopping the line, it also ensures that defects are not created and are passed on to the next stations in the production line. The defect is contained at the station where it was created. This prevents multiple products or batches from having defects.

It is very useful to implement the visual andon and alert systems in every process so that attention can be triggered by the operators who are running those processes in cases of interruptions to their outputs. These andon systems must be supported with a good technician, who can take fast actions and keep the process or machine running effectively. They must know the solutions to minimise the downtime. The usual failure in andon implementation is the help or support system. When the operator triggers the andon, the help is supposed to arrive within seconds or a couple of minutes; but it does not arrive, or the help arrives very late. This poor response will demotivate the operators; and they will stop using the andon, resulting in the failure of the quick problem solving or quick action. What happens when the operator stops using the andon? The output gets impacted because the machine stops and not producing parts, or the machine is running but producing bad parts. In either case, it is bad for the company because it either creates shortages of parts or defects are discovered in the later processes or the final process. By then, it is already too late; throughput constraints are already created in the system.

The andon system must be taken very seriously by everyone in the shop floor, including the area manager. Any failure to respond quickly to an andon light must be treated as a major system failure in the shop floor and be treated very seriously by the organisation's leadership team. The technicians must be well trained with the know-how, experience, and tools to take quick action to processes they are being assigned. It is useless to implement the andon system and not have someone able to respond effectively to solve the problem. The effective andon response system is what normally lacks in many companies.

Value Stream Mapping (VSM)

VSM is the process of carefully studying the activities carried out in the organisation with the objective to create value and to eliminate muda. It is an important tool for the leadership team to reimagine and reconfigure the manufacturing operations to create value across the organisation and the supply chain. VSM also realigns the organisation's workflow (creating value), which is key for organisational intervention and transformation to achieve sustainable competitive business advantage. VSM activity is generally done every year and it is continuous journey to reduce inventories and eliminate NVA activities. The VSM activity is a key driver of many improvements in the organisation: inventories, lead time, throughput, and overall product cost.

This VSM is generally done in a kaizen activity carried out by cross-functional team members. In this VSM kaizen activity, the team will observe and identify all the value-adding and the non-value-adding activities currently done from material delivery to production processes, including completing the product and finally delivering it to the customers. It is done by direct observation and recording of every single activity, the material flowing in the system, production processing, inventories, and WIP. It is looking at the whole picture from ordering raw materials and finally delivering the product to the customer. VSM is a lean tool used to identify all the value-adding and non-value-adding activities and materials by doing a value map of the process from supplier (receiving raw material) to customer (shipping the finished product to customer), highlighting the flow of material, product, information, inventories, waiting, defects, reworks, delays, and all the non-value-adding processes being done in the system. This mapping process is commonly called VSM kaizen or flow kaizen.

In today's businesses, the application of VSM, also referred to as 'visualising the flow' or 'mapping the flow' process, is not limited to the assembly line in production. With proper implementation, VSM fosters a culture of continuous improvement that has been proven effective in manufacturing, information technology, engineering, financial, human resources, legal, and marketing services. Much of lean thinking in knowledge work starts with applying VSM to any work where there are repeatable processes. It must always be done from end to end, not for a single process; it is about looking at the whole business. Although the technical VSM definition varies by industry, its primary concepts have moved beyond manufacturing to be an effective tool for improving processes across all business functions or processes.

VSM is about discovering the non-value-added (NVA) activities, resources and inventories that are present today, called the current state value stream map. Kaizen teams are used to discover those NVAs and find a better method to reduce or eliminate NVAs. Then, the team creates an ideal future-state value stream map, that shows the flow of value, from the start (raw material) to the end (finished product).

VSM activity or VSM kaizen will document every activity, material being used, and materials in the inventories at every process and at every equipment throughout the system. All these types of information (activities and materials) are further analysed and classified as value-adding (for the customer) or non-value-adding for the customer. All materials held in between the process and in the inventories are classified as NVA. The customers do not care about the inventories.

VSM is an important process that every organisation must carry out to establish the amount of NVA that exists in the system and then establish opportunities to reduce those NVA. This is one of the most powerful and easy-to-use mapping tools and can lead the organisation to a rapid and significant improvement to the business performance when the teams implement all actions following the VSM exercise. The total VA and NVA percentage is recorded and established as the baseline for the next VSM kaizen. This VSM process is repeated every six to twelve months. Once all the VSM actions are identified to reduce the NVA, the next step is to implement all the actions (they must be verifiable actions) and ensure they are executed successfully and the gains are captured by constantly auditing the new SOP to ensure new methods are followed.

The organisation leaders must actively and diligently be involved in helping the VSM teams complete the actions on a timely manner. The leadership must take a personal interest in understanding the NVA and to ensure the VSM team is actively implementing the actions, sustaining the results, and doing a weekly or monthly update of status to the leadership team. Any organisation claiming to be in a lean journey but does not actively work on VSM exercise and not focused to reducing NVA is missing the core understanding of lean and TPS strategies.

The figure below shows an example of a nine-step process-flow operations in a product assembly factory. The lead time taken from the time the material preparation was received to the time the products are ready to be shipped out of the factory is 360 minutes versus the actual VA process time of 39 minutes.

Figure 6: Value Stream Mapping (VSM)

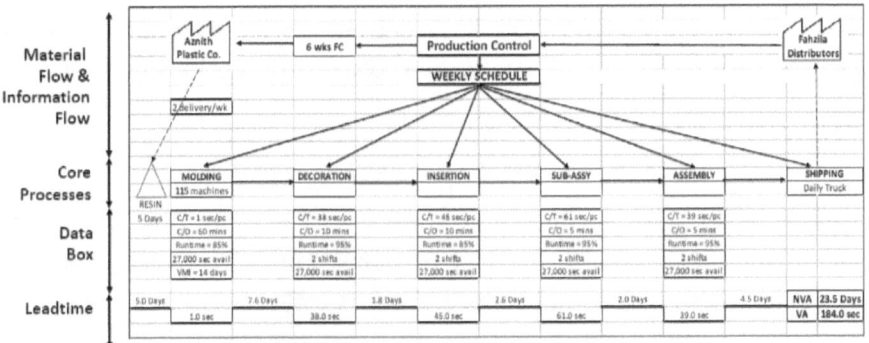

Source: Azlan Nithia, 2018

The VA percentage or the index can be calculated as below:

Total Lead Time (LT) = 360.7 minutes
Total Value-Added (VA) Time = 39.3 minutes
VA index (%) = 360.7 / 39.3 x 100 = 10.8%

It will be shocking for any organisation to discover, after the VSM kaizen is completed, that 90% of the organisation's activities are not adding value to the product or to the consumer. Most of the companies will be equally shocked to discover that a VSM kaizen exercise will reveal that their VA is less than 5%. These are common VSM discoveries. These results must be positively viewed as a big opportunity to improve the current performance, especially in inventories, rework, lead time, throughput, quality, and cost.

The VA percentage or the VA index is a good indication of the opportunity that exists in the system currently, and the organisation must seriously focus to reduce the NVA activities in the whole system. Most often, organisations make a big mistake by improving the VA portion of the processes; but instead, the focus must be to reduce the NVA activities (this is the waste or muda). The VA is what the customer is willing to pay for. An example is transporting the parts from machine A to machine B. It is obvious that there is no change to the product form, so this is classified as NVA. By keeping the parts in the inventory, there is no change to the product; so again, it is classified as NVA. Similarly, reworking a defective part is NVA. These are the activities that the customer is not willing to pay for, and the customer does not see their value in the product.

The parts that are held in the inventory or storage or WIP are all considered as NVA because it is a waste to keep parts in the storage and inventory, it delays the flow of parts, and it results in a longer lead time. The first step to reduce NVA is to focus on decreasing the inventory quantities (reduce them or most preferred is to eliminate where possible) at every process. If a buffer inventory is required to manage certain constraints in the system, then there must be a very good reason, such as to reduce the bottleneck in the next process or improve the flow. Any kind of storage of parts or materials in the inventory holding must be done with a kanban visual control system and with the minimum-maximum quantity inventory control, which is established strictly to meet OTIF customer deliveries. The organisation must be highly concerned with any kind of inventory holding in the manufacturing system. This is extremely important to ensure the production is operating with the smallest lot size or batch size, with a lot size of one being the ultimate goal. The lean concept encourages manufacturing operations to continuously strive towards achieving the one-piece flow as a relentless improvement journey to achieve excellence in manufacturing. It requires the continuous reduction of the inventories in the manufacturing processes to improve the flow and to reduce lot size.

The VSM process should be repeated every six months (or at least once a year). All the improvement activities must be driven from the

VSM outcome. After the VSM kaizen is completed, clear improvement objectives must be established. This is how more kaizen events are organised to realise the results expected from the VSM kaizen. All related actions must be tracked and ensure implementation and the results realised as committed during the VSM kaizen exercise. The organisation should assign teams to implement all the improvement actions. This must be done in a well-organised kaizen workshops to focus on the ideas for the improvement. These actions must be implemented using the kaizen approach. Organisations must track all the actions through an activity called make-daily-improvements (MDI) activity.

CHAPTER 3

The Journey for Continuous Improvement

Early Detection and Immediate Action

The concept of 3 NDs (no defects) are the following:

1. Make no defects (make good parts)
2. Send no defects (send good parts)
3. Receive no defects (receive good parts)

These 3 NDs must be developed into an operational culture, instilled in everyone in the shop floor, and the employees must be empowered to practise this without any fear. This culture of 3 NDs cultivates the system of early detection and immediate action, which will result in preventing defects being made. This prevents mura, muri, and muda. In any manufacturing industry, the concept of early detection, immediate action, and prevention of defects from happening again is an important quality mindset required for a high-performing organisation. The A3 problem-solving process must be imbedded into the organisation's DNA.

Early detection + immediate action = defect prevention

The Pride of Workmanship

There must be a clear flow of problem solving. Operators need to have a complete understanding of normal conditions. Whenever there is a gap, they know there is a problem. The operators or the technicians must learn to see the parts and the equipment they are using and able to recognise when they have a problem. The first indication is when a part is defective. It means something is going wrong in the process. The operators and technicians must know if the conditions are normal or not. To know this, they must be knowledgeable of what is abnormal condition and empowered to immediately stop the machine from making any defective part. The core requirement of implementing pride of workmanship is to empower the operators and technicians to take immediate action and to stop the production line or the machine whenever a defective part or an abnormal condition is found.

The 3 NDs are an important work culture that cultivate the pride of workmanship in every employee. The employee must have pride in what they do and deliver to the next process. This pride of workmanship culture applies to both manufacturing and administrative processes, as well as the whole organisation. The employee who is doing the work has the responsibility to not make a defect. If the process or the method is not capable to make a good part, the employee must quickly raise the andon for help and stop making and defective parts (do not make defects).

In case a defective part is made, then it is the responsibility of the employee to identify those defective parts and label them as defective. Those defective parts cannot flow to the next process until those parts was reworked and confirmed as good part at the station where the defect was created. The containment of defective parts at the source is extremely important (do not send defects). If a defective part is moved to the next subsequent process, it only creates NVA work carried out on a defective part. Ultimately, these defective parts would require a lot more rework in the next process or may have to be rejected (beyond rework). The employees must be trained, or the process inputs must be designed (mistake proofing) so that it is possible to detect any defective part coming into the process (do not receive defect).

When a manufacturing or production group is highly focused on output, measured by the number of units made by a process and highly driven by the quantity to deliver every shift, this will drive the work behaviour of 'quantity first and quality second'. This behaviour will exist in the shop floor as an unspoken way of doing things in production areas. It is very bad for the organisation because it gives the impression that the company is only interested in the quantity. In this kind of work environment, the workers and supervisors are recognised for the quantity they deliver. The defective parts sent to the next process will continue till the final process is completed. Then, the quality inspection will catch them, and then they are rejected at the end process.

This is also the reason measuring local efficiency and individual process efficiency is not effective. It drives poor employee behaviour at workplace and negatively impacts the teamwork driven by common goals.

So who is responsible for those defective parts? Who is that somebody who made it? Will we know where and when the defect was created? Do we know how many defects were created and how many production lots are now contaminated with this defect? A common problem in many companies is the lack of pride of workmanship.

To instil the 3 NDs is not an easy task. It requires a new workplace culture. Start with one ND at a time. Start with the first (do not make defects). This will require an effective andon light or siren system, quick response from the technicians to solve the problems quickly, and strong commitment from the front-line leadership. If this first ND is not effectively implemented, then the other two NDs will fail. An immediate action must be taken as soon as a defect was detected by the operator. The first step is to support the process or the machine that is making the defects and then immediately trigger the andon for help.

This is the seven-step sequence of events when a defective part is produced and detected:

1. A defective part is detected by the operator.
2. The operator immediately stops the machine or the process that is making the defect.
3. The operator triggers the andon for help.
4. The operator isolates those defective parts produced from the good parts.
5. The technician arrives quickly (within seconds or minutes) and solves the problem, confirms the process and machine is capable to produce good parts, and hands over the machine to the operator.
6. The operator starts running the machine and produces good parts.
7. The front-line leader decides what action needs to be taken to rectify those defective parts produced.

The above is an example of a good manufacturing practice that is required in the shop floor to operationalise the behaviour of 'early detection, immediate action'. This is one of the important people behaviour and engagement that must be cultivated to achieve manufacturing excellence. For a non-defective condition, establish what needs to be inspected.

It is extremely critical to ensure that the engineers responsible for the machines and the processes are deeply engaged in the daily production performance monitoring for any new machine or process being released to production. There must be a system or procedure in place that holds the engineers accountable for 'clean releases' of machines and processes to production and complete the daily tracking till the machine and process achieves consistent quality and output performances. I have come across numerous companies whereby the engineers would release the machine and process to the production operator while its performance is still very questionable. This imposes a heavy burden on the operator and the production staffs to meet the expected quality and hourly outputs. Therefore, it is important to have a procedure that requires production personnel involvement in every machine and process design, as well as a buy-off and handover procedure between the engineers and the production personnel.

The Concept of Jidoka

The term *jidoka* (a Japanese word) is used in the TPS and can be defined as the 'automation with a human touch'. The word *jidoka* traces its roots to the invention of the automatic loom by Sakichi Toyoda, the founder of the Toyota Group. The automatic loom is a machine that spins thread for cloth and weaves textiles automatically.

Before automated devices were commonplace, back-strap looms, ground looms, and high-warp looms were used to manually weave cloth. In 1896, Sakichi Toyoda invented Japan's first self-powered loom called the Toyoda power loom. Subsequently, he incorporated numerous revolutionary inventions into his looms, including the weft-breakage automatic stopping device (which automatically stopped the loom when a thread breakage was detected), the warp supply device, and the automatic shuttle changer. Then, in 1924, Sakichi invented the world's first automatic loom called the type-G Toyoda automatic loom (with nonstop shuttle-change motion), which could change shuttles without stopping operation. (This is the concept of zero loss time during changeovers.)

The Toyota term *jido* is applied to a machine with a built-in device for making judgements whereas the regular Japanese term *jido* (automation) is simply applied to a machine that moves on its own. Jidoka refers to automation with a human touch as opposed to a machine that simply moves under the monitoring and supervision of an operator. Since the loom stopped when a problem arose, no defective products were produced. This meant that a single operator could be put in charge of numerous looms, resulting in a tremendous improvement in productivity.

The concept of jidoka is one of the core pillars of TPS and helps to stop and fix the problems. At Toyota, this translates into the andon, a cord hanging above the production line. Whenever an employee encounters a problem, the cord is pulled, and the production line is stopped. All employees in the line know that a problem has occurred. A visual or alarm sound system is triggered, telling them where the problem occurred. With the line being stopped, the employees can focus to immediately solving the problem. By stopping the line, it also ensures that defects are not passed onto the next stations in the production line. The defect is contained at the station where it was created. This prevents multiple products or batches becoming defective, and immediate action is taken to rectify the problem (early detection, immediate action).

Jidoka's Four-Step Approach

   i. Detect the deviation from the specification or the SOP.
   ii. Immediately stop the production line.
   iii. Act quickly to fix the problem and start the line.
   iv. Analyse the root cause of the problem and implement preventive actions so that the same problem will not recur.

Since the equipment stops when a problem arises, the operator can visually monitor and efficiently control many machines. To surface the problem, it is important to use a "visual problem display board". It should be located it in the shop floor. This visual boards, also called the andon board, allows the operators to identify the problems in the production lines (machines and processes) and show it in the visual andon board.

It is important that the operational system is adequately developed and executes the early detection and immediate action all the time. The employees and the technicians must be well trained, equipped, and capable to practise this jidoka system of early detection and immediate action all the time. The employee culture of early detection and immediate action can happen only if the employees are good at problem solving or have the ability to take immediate corrective actions to keep the process or the machine running with good parts with very little downtime or loss time.

Make Daily Improvements (MDI)

Most often, companies claim kaizen outcome or results cannot be sustained, lean journey failure, can fail, and many other reasons. These failures to sustain the gains can always be traced back to the failure of execution. The MDI activity is an extremely important exercise to ensure all the kaizen actions are implemented effectively and efficiently. It involves the responsible process owners. The kaizen team must audit the area and processes daily with the process owners to ensure all actions are implemented as planned and to get the employee feedback for any adjustments to the implementation plan. This is the meaning of making daily improvements.

The kaizen improvements can fail and cannot be sustained due to the failure of not doing the MDI activity. An organisation should create a gemba culture, a culture whereby the management team is willing and happy to walk the shop floor daily. The product value is created in the production processes (in the shop floor) and not in the offices.

The management team must take serious interest to support the teams and to ensure every kaizen action item is effectively implemented and delivers the results. A weekly review or a thirty-minute update by the kaizen team to the management team must be made compulsory for both the kaizen team and the management team. These weekly kaizen update meetings must start sharp on time and finish on time to show commitment and discipline. Starting the meeting late and finishing it late indicates that these update meetings are not important and not well organised.

Daily, walk the shop floor and observe the new work method. Look for deviations or difficulties being faced by the employees with the new work method. Encourage the employees to record the difficulties they faced. Make corrective actions and improve ideas. It is recommended to provide a visual board or flip chart at the work area so that the employees can write their ideas down, and it is visual. This is called the

MDI kaizen newspaper. Look for ways to help the employees to solve these problems immediately.

For example, the process engineer must walk the shop floor to review the performance of the processes that he or she is in charge of. Constantly look for process improvements. Equally important is safety (including environment and health conditions in the area). However small it can be, look for the improvements.

The supervisors, managers, and organisation's general manager must set the example to walk the shop floor daily and ask the employees for the problem of the day and how it was solved. What about the human resources manager? Where are the people that they are serving? As we know, they are mostly in the shop floor. How often does the human resources team walk to the shop floor? It is about creating a new organisation culture and to operationalise a new set of people behaviour.

Sustaining versus Continuous Improvement

The biggest and most difficult task in any transformation or improvement programme or after a kaizen event is to sustain the gains. Most of the lean and kaizen improvements evaporate very quickly. Some even are lost as quickly as a week or two after the improvement kaizen event.

The discussion of sustaining improvements and gains is a hot topic amongst the leaders in many organisations in the lean journey. Leaders very often complain that they are not able to retain the improvements. Therefore, there's a need to re-kaizen or the need to regroup the team to redo the activities again and again.

Question:

- Why is sustaining the improvement important?
- Why not continuously focus on improving instead of sustaining?

Figure 7: Sustainable Continuous Improvement—the Journey

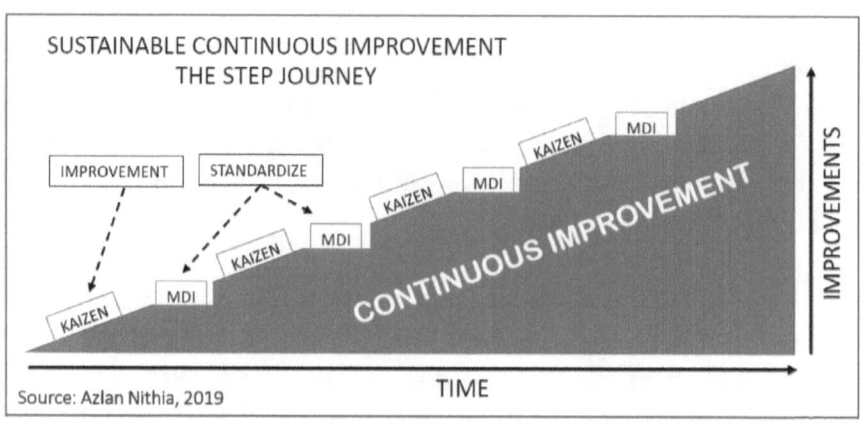

I have personally seen numerous organisations struggling to sustain the improvements year on year. The performance slides backwards down to the old performance; the improved results cannot be sustained. The leaders have lots of reasons and excuses. Most often, they will blame their own people for their poor follow-up and lack of commitment.

If you and your team truly believe in continuous improvement as an organisational work culture, then why sustain a performance standard? Instead of sustaining, why not drive continuous improvement, including small or incremental improvements (micro-improvements)? The danger of sustaining is sliding backwards, but the power of small incremental improvements means moving forward. Therefore, sustaining the improvements becomes a spin-off of the concept of continuously improving.

> Sustaining = Not moving up or down (stationary)
> Continuous Improvement = Always going up (improving)
> Manufacturing excellence's 'weapon' is continuous improvement.

Think of micro-improvements instead of sustaining (the improvements). Sustaining means you are stationary and not moving. It can only possibly move down if the performance is being sustained.

Why operationalise micro-improvements after an improvement has been made? It simply means small incremental improvements daily on the process that was improved or kaizen. This is also the reason MDI is extremely important to ensure all the improvements will not slide backwards. The MDI Team is formed immediately after a Kaizen event is completed. The MDI Team is formed immediately after a Kaizen event is completed. This MDI Team will meet daily, go to the Gemba (shop floor) where the improvements was made during the Kaizen. The objective of this team is to look for improvements (daily) and to ensure the new SOP is understood and followed. Then, expand the good practices to others processes. This MDI process must go on for the next thirty days. Those who are in charge or responsible for the process area must do the daily gemba observation with the kaizen team members. During this period, clear SOPs must be developed, all the requirements must be completed, and consistent performance and results must be achieved daily and every hour.

Continuous improvement is the most powerful manufacturing excellence weapon. This must be embedded as the organisation's DNA and a daily work culture across the whole organisation. Everyone walks the talk of continuous improvement in every work they do, demonstrating that every day is a better day.

CHAPTER 4

Organisation and People Culture

Manufacturing Excellence 3M House

The struggle that many organisations face is not in where to apply lean or the agile tools but how to effect the organisational and behavioural change required for a successful transformation. The new change in organisational performance will not happen if the people culture remains the same because it is the people who impact the change. The manufacturing excellence 3M house explains the core foundation (people culture) that is required to continuously reduce the 3M wastes in manufacturing to achieve manufacturing excellence. The organisation's people culture and their capability to impact change is the core foundation for achieving manufacturing excellence.

However, while embarking on a transformation journey using lean methods, many organisations fail to realise that without a change of culture, the lean methods or manufacturing excellence are unlikely to be successfully adopted and contribute business value. Lean method or lean manufacturing is not a programme or a set of tools, but it is about transforming an organisation's culture. It is about leadership commitment. It is a relentless journey without a finishing line and a pursuit for continuous improvement. Often, organisations fail to articulate a compelling vision for this change, one that can be consistently communicated to the employees and readily internalised by everyone at all levels.

What is manufacturing excellence? What do the manufacturing excellence experts say about the organisations that are serious about achieving the manufacturing excellence?

Larry E. East, in his book *The 12 Principles of Manufacturing Excellence*, says it is not the flavour of the month. It is continuous improvement (CI). It is forever. It must be the operating strategy for the business.

Andrew Miller, in his book *Redefining Operational Excellence: New Strategies for Maximum Performance and Profits Across the Organization*, says operational excellence is the relentless pursuit of doing things better. It is not a destination or a methodology but a mindset that needs to exist across an organisation. It is about empowering employees to use judgement on the front lines.

The numerous cost-reduction programmes are usually launched to achieve transformational initiatives that would apply lean methodology to reduce costs and process complexity and eliminate waste from the system. The complexities involved in managing lean transformation programmes have made the success rate or the sustaining to be poor, especially the ability to sustain the lean gains. The key reason for the low success rate is that many organisations deploying lean manufacturing use them as a tool to achieve cost reductions, which is their only primary objective. The decisions made by the leaders very often overlook the organisational, behavioural, and cultural aspects of this lean transformation. The leadership team must understand that people culture and engagement play a very critical role in the success of lean adoption as an organisational culture and the achievement of an organisational ambience for other transformational programmes to succeed.

It is all about the leadership team's commitment and the people's engagement to drive improvements and create them as an organization's new work culture at all levels.

People Culture Is the Foundation

The future of manufacturing is rapidly changing, transforming into a digitally powered automated manufacturing environment that will require highly skilled talents and becoming lesser labour-intensive operations. Therefore, the skills needed are changing. It requires the ability to manage complex tasks, to constantly learn, and to apply new knowledge.

The kaizen philosophy requires the step-by-step improvements, process refinements, and continuous enhancements, which are the surest and fastest route to achieving optimum productivity gains and quality improvements. Making small step improvements, done in many processes, will lead to accumulated significant improvements in productivity, quality, lead time, and cost.

Figure 8: Manufacturing Excellence—3M House

Figure 9: Manufacturing Excellence's 3M House

Source: Azlan Nithia, 2018

The change and improvements will be an ongoing process. It is good to establish a reliable change process communication system in the organisation. The only thing that will not stop changing is the change itself. The best change is one initiated by the people. High involvement is good but never overlain cumbersome, and it should not interfere with the people to be successful in their regular function or role.

People usually will not mind new changes made in the workplace if they are used to the idea that the management will always give them an opportunity to be involved, and they too have an impact on the direction of the change. It can even be as minor as asking the people for their opinions on the new direction or the new change. This will improve the participation level and involvement of the people to execute the new direction from its early implementation stage to full implementation.

It is all about talking to the people, communicating to them openly (have a structure of how this communication will be done at all levels in the organisation) and letting the people feel that they are part of the new change process. It is important to recognise that under every successful new change implementation, there is a lot of hard work; and it has a lot to do with good and effective communication.

Develop the measurement systems and add them into the change process that visually tells the performance to the people, indicating when they are making progress or not based on the new revised targets. There must be full alignment, which includes the consequences of not following the new SOP and rewards for those positively delivering good results.

Creating a work environment in which employees feel as if they have the power to initiate change is also positive and a tribute to your work culture. But more frequently, employees find themselves caught up in changes that others are initiating.

The innovation-and automation-minded managers generally are quick to resort to buying new automated machines and robots to create islands of improvements; but it may not create total system value or actual enhancement in end-to-end productivity gains. It may, in fact, impede changeovers and reduce flexibility. Leaning out the processes through a VSM kaizen should always be the priority. Remove the 3M wastes first, and the implementation of automation or robotics should be last; if not, the engineers would have only automated lots of NVA waste.

The key to achieve manufacturing excellence in the competitive business environment is by having the right people and organisation culture that is always ready to learn and apply, able to deal with complex challenges and constantly improving. To adapt and manage change effectively, continually realigning and reassessing the organisation's people culture is crucial. It is all about the people and the organisation's agility that is required to drive CIs and to create change for the better.

The continuous advancements in industrial technologies requires the constant upgrading of the people talent and skills. It is important to develop a learning organisation that can adapt quickly to the changing technological requirements.

The organisations need to seriously consider people talents:

1. Good presentation skills and the ability to articulate new ideas effectively and quickly
2. Creativity and ability to solve problems effectively and generate creative solutions
3. Ability to critically analyse and think through the various options to develop better ways of doing work
4. Ability to autonomously work with digitally connected systems, machines, and digital feedback outputs to make decisions as the organisations embrace and implement the requirements of smart factories
5. Capable of teamwork and working across various functions to efficiently complete the task, be very agile to work on multiple processes, and be adaptable to the changing customer requirements
6. Responsible, accountable, and hardworking in seeking constant improvements

A human resources (HR) team that understands the importance of the above effectively provides the support to make it happen.

The manufacturing house (3M wastes) consists of the two very important people foundations:

- CI (and learning)—everyday a better day
- Daily gemba kaizen, jidoka, and problem solving

Then, on those two core people foundations are the three key pillars of 3M:

- Muda waste (to discover, reduce, and eliminate)
- Mura unevenness (to discover, reduce, and eliminate)
- Muri overburden (to discover, reduce, and eliminate)

On top of these three 3M pillars (muda, mura, and muri) sits the activities, which are to constantly identify, reduce, or eliminate all the 3M wastes in all the processes and activities. Finally, it creates the outcome that leads the organisation to achieve manufacturing excellence.

The Four Key People Culture Foundations

There are four key foundations that must be developed and operationalised as an organisational people culture (like the company DNA). These four components form the core requirements for any high-performing organisation to be successful in implementing the smart manufacturing and the factories of the future. This foundational culture will ensure a sustainable business growth, profitability, and leadership in the industry.

1. Continuous Improvement

Employees in the organisation must practise the work culture of continuously improving the processes and be engaged in the daily improvement activities. It is important for the organisation to embrace, cultivate the learning culture, and ensure that every employee is engaged in finding new knowledge and implementing new ideas to enhance performance.

The concept of every day a better day is the key of continuous learning and CI. This is a work culture that must become the core foundation for all the employees and the management team in the organisation. If this is not developed or operationalised, then every other improvement programmes will not stick and cannot sustain the gains or improvements. The improvements will be lost very quickly after any kaizen event is completed.

2. Problem-solving Culture

There must be a daily activity to find the problem, highlight them and take immediate corrective action. Problem solving must be practised at all levels. The ability to effectively and quickly solve problems is a key requirement of a high-performing organisation, team, and employee. If the organisation does not have teams and employees who can effectively and quickly solve daily chronic problems, it is not possible to achieve high performance. Quality improvement and effective problem solving are the key requirements to be successful in any industry. The quality improvement process is an endless journey, continuously pursuing the goal of zero defect or perfection.

Therefore, it is important that the employees are engaged in daily activities to constantly improve quality by identifying problems and using a simple A3 methodology to systematically solve the problem and prevent the problems from recurring. The goal should be to solve the day's problem within the same day. It is important to visually track the percentage of the problems solved within the same day (strive towards 100%) and review it the next day during the daily gemba problem-solving activity (should be conducted early in the work shift). These daily problems must be tracked and recorded in the kaizen newspaper, a flip chart that is used to write down the problems and to show the immediate actions that were taken to solve them (located at process). These problems must also be tracked to ensure they are not repeated problems. For those repeated problems, an A3 problem-solving kaizen must be conducted to further break down the problem, find the root cause, and implement the actions to prevent them from happening or occurring again. This is the team's relentless focus to ensure the same will not be repeated.

The A3-DD Methodology for Problem Solving

Problem solving must be made simple so that everyone in the organisation can solve problems quickly and effectively. There are numerous problem-solving tools available in the market. Normally, they require very lengthy and completed processes to find the root causes or to solve the problem. As a result, most often companies will assign one or two highly trained individuals especially trained to use these complex problem-solving tools or methodologies. This kind of complex approach to solving a problem should not be encouraged. It is also very common for engineers to immediately jump into the causes. This is wrong and will result in difficulty to solve the problem permanently. Those engineers who have been working in the area may think they know it all and may also use their past knowledge to solve the current problems. This is a dangerous behaviour towards problem solving. Every problem must be taken very seriously. One must always establish the root cause very precisely, and preventive actions must be completed to ensure the same problem will not repeat again.

It is important to define the problem correctly. The way you define the problem will determine how it will be solved. There are big problems will many variables, and there are also the small production problems, which need to be solved quickly. The big problems (generally with several variables) may require more time and effort to solve. The big problems should be converted into a problem-solving kaizen event and turned into a regular kaizen project.

The simplest and most effective problem-solving methodology that I have personally used, which helped successfully solve hundreds of problems, is called the DD. This is a globally proven and powerful approach towards solving any kind of quality problems. This methodology is also known as DD. The founder of this DD methodology for solving quality problems was Professor Dr Shrinivas Gondhalekar (aka Dr G). Dr G introduced his DD methodology in the book titled *Chronicles of a Quality Detective—Developing Differential Diagnosis: A Powerful Approach Towards Solving Quality Problems* (Gondhalekar, 2005). This DD approach has also been successfully used in solving various kinds of administrative-related problems.

I have personally used this DD methodology for more than fifteen years to solve various problems, and I have found this method to be the simplest approach that can be easily adopted companywide by everyone. This method also facilitates quick problem solving.

Most often, engineers and problem solvers focus on why the defect occurred; therefore, they spend lot of time and resources analysing the defective parts or the item with the defect. In most cases, the defect percentage will be very low, in the region of 5% to 10%, as the good parts or parts without any defects are more than 90%. This is how most of the problem-solving approaches work. Therefore, this has become a natural problem-solving behaviour used by engineers in most of the organisations.

By only looking at the defective parts, I have found the it is very time-consuming to finally get to the root cause. As a result, organisations deploys very complex and sophisticated problem-solving methodologies. This had required certain individuals to be especially trained and become a problem-solving experts in the company. I have found this approach of having only one or two experts to solve problems to be very unproductive because problem solving must be everyone's responsibility and not confined to certain experts only. To become a high-performing individual and a high-performing organisation, the problem-solving skills are critical.

Figure 9: Focus on Why Parts Are Good

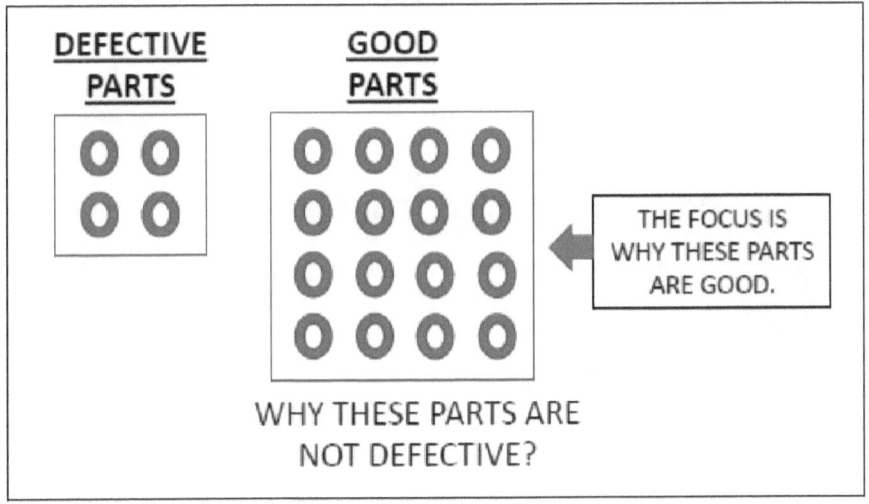

Source: Azlan Nithia, 2019

A Problem-Solving Case Study

One of the processes in a company (let us name it Company A) used for this case study is called the 'load, punch, and cap assembly' process that produces a PVC part with a cap. It was having lots of missing production orders. The production supervisor was complaining that fewer than 70% were good. This was after a lot of rework. It also required many rework operators. There were four machines, and each machine loaded the part, punched a hole, assembled the cap, and finally unloaded the part. The general manager of this factory had approved to replace all these four machines based on the equipment engineer's recommendation. The reason for replacement was justified as these four machines were over 5 years old. They produced too many defects, increased the production costs, and lowered the productivity of this operation. The company was missing the customer orders, and the situation had reached a serious level due to the delivery shortages and many customer complaints.

Figure 10: PVC Part Load, Punch, and Cap Assembly Machine

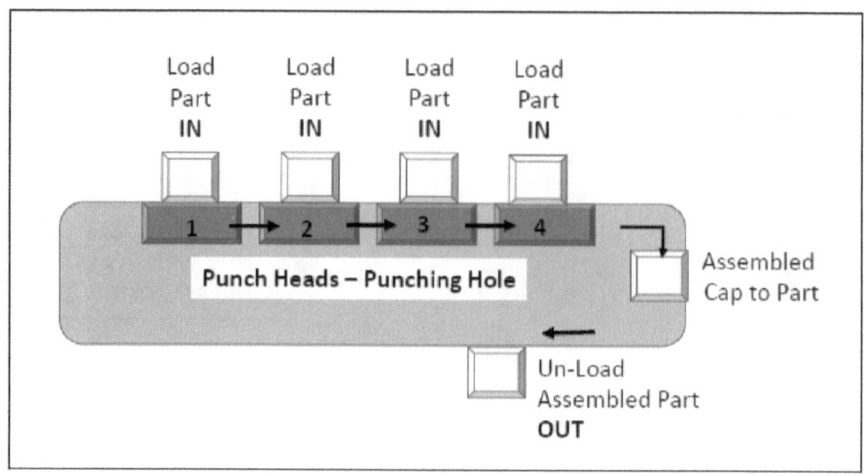

Source: Azlan Nithia, 2019

I had volunteered to investigate this problem and attempted to solve this defective-parts problem at all these four machines. I requested for a day to review the situation and give my recommendations. Meanwhile, I had requested the general manager to put his decision to buy new machines on hold.

The approach used are as follows:

Step 1: Define the Problem

The first and the most important step to define the problem precisely. The accurate problem definition is the key to successful problem solving.

The defect was defined as the excess material on the part after punching (at the edges around the hole). This excess material was not acceptable and had to be removed manually after the punching and cap assembly process, which was done at another rework station.

The defect was the excess material at the edges around the hole; and if there was no excess material around the hole, it was considered as a good part. The problem definition is defined as the *gap between the expected target results versus the current actual results*. The gap between these two (target versus current) is the problem. If this gap is closed, and the target equals the actual then, there is no problem.

The defects could be reworked manually, but they required extra time and operators. The rework process was not easy, and it was producing between 20% and 30% defects (those that cannot be reworked).

Figure 11: The Gap Equals to Problem

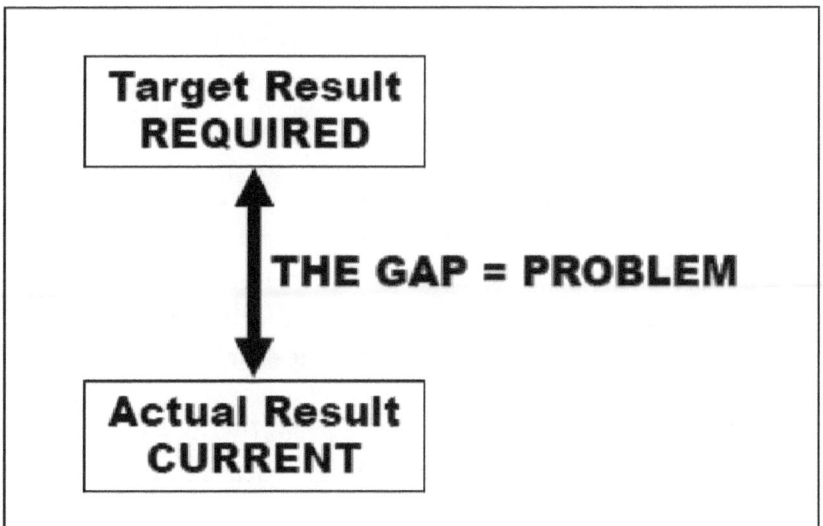

Source: Azlan Nithia, 2019

Step 2: Locate Where the Defect Is Present and Absent

The defect was only present around the hole areas, and it was absent at all other areas. The defect was discovered at all four machines; but it was only at machine 1 and the punch heads 2 and 4 that the parts were found to be good. Punch heads 1 and 3 were found to have defective parts (excess material around the hole).

3. Identify the Process Where the Defect Is Present and Absent

The defect was only present after the punch-head process, and no other defects were created at any other process. Therefore, the conclusion was made that the defects were found only after punching the hole at the punch-head process.

I observed all the four punching machines and looked at all the parts from each punching head. There were a total of four machines, and each machine had four punch heads. Therefore, the total were sixteen punch heads, with two making good parts and fourteen making defective parts with excess material. I also discussed with the machine operator to get inputs from the operators regarding their observations about which were making good and bad parts. It is important to have a discussion with those directly involved in the process. This allows me to gather additional information that may assist in solving the problem.

Each machine had four punching heads. Each punching head punched one part at a time. All the punching heads were in one straight line. All were punching at the same time. Therefore, one machine could produce four parts per punching cycle. Each machine was operated by one operator. The four machines' performances are as below:

- **Machine 1:** This machine had two heads (heads 2 and 4) making good parts and the other two heads (heads 1 and 3) making defective parts.
- **Machine 2:** This machine had all four heads making defective parts.
- **Machine 3:** This machine had all four heads making defective parts.
- **Machine 4:** This machine had all four heads making defective parts.

Step 4: Compare the Good and the Defective Parts

I compared the machines and punch heads that were producing good parts and defective parts (with excess material around the hole). Machine 1 with punch heads 2 and 4 were making good parts. All other punch heads were making defective parts (the hole had excess material). The question that I needed to ask was, why were machine 1's punch heads 2 and 4 making good parts? The focus was now required only on the punch-head process because step 3 had indicated that the defect was present immediately after the punch-head process.

I asked the operator managing the machine 1 if anything was done by anyone to the heads 2 and 4. The operator showed me the maintenance record book and pointed to the work that was done by a maintenance technician to head 2 and, later, to head 4. When I reviewed the book, it indicated that the technician replaced the punch cutter on head 2; and later he changed the punch cutter on head 4.

The next step was to speak to the technician who changed the punch cutter on heads 2 and 4. I had a discussion with the technician and confirmed he changed the punch cutters in punch heads 2 and 4. The reason he changed them was because the cutter was cracked and could not do the punching process. This was an important information. The technician attached new punch cutters to heads 2 and 4. This confirmed that, after changing to new punch cutters, the defect related to excess material at the hole disappeared at punch heads 2 and 4. It was always important establish the clue. In this particular case, punch heads 2 and 4 had new punch cutters.

I spoke to technician and the operators managing the four machines. I asked if they would allow me to replace the punch cutters on machine 1, particularly on punch heads 1 and 3. After having the agreement, I requested that machine 1 be stopped. I removed the current punch cutters on heads 1 and 3 and replaced them with new punch cutters. It was a fast twenty-minute job. After testing the function of the new punch cutters, the technician restarted machine 1, now with new punch cutters on heads 1 and 3. The result was amazing. The heads 1 and 3 produced clean holes without any excess material around the holes.

Next, I repeated the solution to the rest of the machines. After about one hour, all the machines' punch cutters were replaced; and the process started running again. All the machines were re-inspected and reconfirmed by the quality inspector, the technician, and the operator. All of them confirmed that all parts from all four machines were acceptable and good parts. There was no more excess material around the hole. This means the rework process could be stopped and the operators currently doing the hole rework could be deployed to other useful work. I can now confirm that the problem is solved, and I can also recreate the defect because I now know the root cause to the problem. I continued to observe all the four machines for another one hour to ensure the operator, technician, and the quality inspectors were all satisfied and confirmed the problem was now solved.

Step 5: Create a Preventive Action to Ensure the Same Problem Will Not Occur Again

This is an important step to ensure the problem will not recur. This will require a new SOP that will drive a new work procedure to prevent the same defect from recurring. The new SOP will ensure that the punch cutters are inspected by the technician every shift to confirm they are in good operating condition and the operator checks it every hour. The punch cutter quality specification is also determined and added to the SOP along with the weekly PM schedule for the punch heads in all the four machines.

Figure 12: The Five-Step Problem-Solving Approach

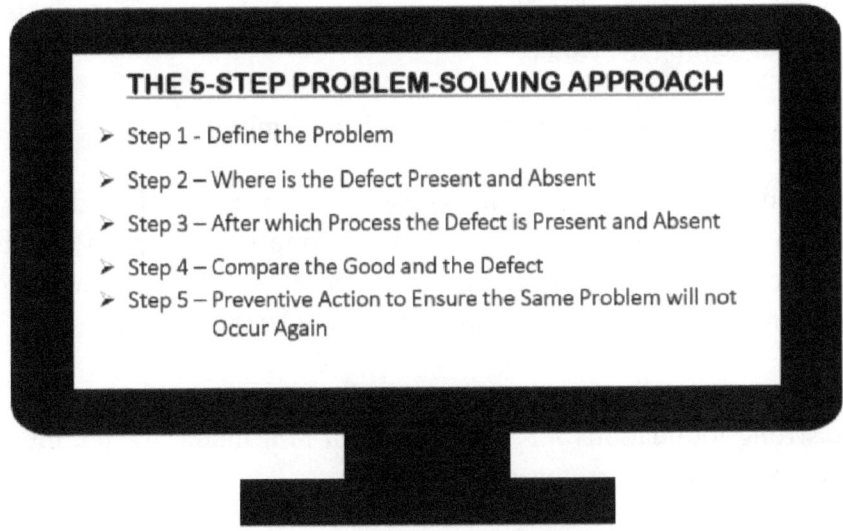

The above explains the five-step approach that solved the problem and will prevent the problem from occurring again. The general manager confirmed that the machines are operating well and producing good parts. The purchase of the new machines was cancelled.

4. The Daily Gemba Kaizen

This is the 'small group-kaizen activity' or SG-KA. Daily, the SG-KA team will walk and observe the work area to find opportunities to improve and take immediate actions to implement those improvements. This is done daily by the area's SG-KA team. The SG-KA team members are selected from the line operators, line leaders, technicians, and quality personnel. This daily gemba kaizen is normally done during the beginning of the work shift for about twenty minutes, and then the team regroups to discuss the improvements and what actions to be taken, and by whom and when. These improvements are tracked and reviewed daily to ensure successful implementation.

Generally, these are small improvements implemented daily. If the team finds a bigger improvement opportunity, which is beyond the team's ability to implement, then the supervisor or the area manager will get involved, helping the team.

5. Constant Improvement of Jidoka (Visual Andon)

Stop and fix the problems. Do not make defects, do not send the defects, and do not receive the defects. A good shop-floor response team (technicians and line leaders) must be deployed to ensure problems are fixed immediately when an andon is triggered by the operator.

The above four people cultures are the key foundations. They sit as the strong foundations for three pillars of 3M: muda (waste), mura (unevenness), and muri (overburdened).

The Four Key People Culture Foundations

- Continuous improvement—every day a better day
- Daily problem solving—simple and effective (A3)
- Daily gemba kaizen (SG-KA)
- Constant improvement of jidoka (visual andon system and response time)

The above four cultures must be developed, cultivated, nourished and relentlessly reinforced as an organisational culture, which is the way we do business and how we work. This must apply across the whole organisation, particularly across all the functions in manufacturing and business processes.

Only by relentlessly pursuing and achieving all the key people concepts and making these concepts as part of the organisation's imbedded DNA can an organisation realise manufacturing excellence, constantly reducing lead time, reducing product cost, and improving throughput and productivity.

Visual Performance Management (VPM)

In every work area, it is important to create the awareness of the area's performance by using visual displays. This enables the employees in that process area and for the management team to see the area's performance visually during the Gemba walk (or the shop-floor walk). The visual charts will show the current performance status and the targeted performance. It provides a visual feedback to the employees and ownership of the results (good or bad). These visual boards will also show any action taken to mitigate any problem that had arisen or issues unsolved requiring supervisor intervention. It also supplements the 5S process of visual workplace and visual flow.

VPM provides real-time information on process performance so that immediate actions are taken, and this enables CI and quick problem solving to ensure problems do not prolong or carry over to the next shift. Quick response to resolve any problem in the shop floor is extremely critical.

The VPM must also ensure the visual material flow in the production shop floor. Every material flow must be clearly identified. Some examples of material flow visual identifications (MFVI) required are the following:

1. Raw material input
2. Input (to a process)
3. Accepted and rejected material
4. Material that requires rework
5. Material pending quality decision
6. Output accepted and completed
7. Every inventory (small or large) with is kanban system (minimum and maximum inventory levels allowed; no inventory is allowed without a kanban)

The following are the daily and weekly activities that are keys for VPM implementation and to effective improvements:

- **Operators**—visual recording of hourly production data, production interruptions, material shortages, and equipment stoppage time
- **Front-line leaders**—end-of-shift meeting with operators at the production visual performance board to review output and any issues and prioritise improvement activities for the next shift
- **Managers**—morning meeting with the leaders at the production visual performance board to ensure availability of resources required for solving problems and those requiring management help
- **General manager**—weekly meeting with department managers at the production visual performance board to review the week's performance, problems solved, preventive action taken, improvement of ideas, and those requiring management help or support.

The supporting departments such as maintenance, quality, engineering, procurement, HR, and administration team members should join the managers and the general manager.

Figure 13: Visual Performance Management

VISUAL PERFORMANCE BOARD					
PEOPLE	PERFORMANCE			PROBLEM SOLVING	
SAFETY	QUALITY	OUTPUT	LOTS MISSED		
IMPROV IDEAS					
	MATERIAL FLOW & MACHINE PERFORMANCE			MGMT ATTENTION	
5S SCORE	MATL DELAYS	EQ STOPS	OEE		

Source: Azlan Nithia, 2019

The management team should decide the critical charts or measurements that must be visually displayed in the VPM board. These VPM boards can be manually managed by the area employees or digitally managed by using large monitors. VPM must be kept very simple with very little words on it, but it has more of the visual performance trends and graphs to show whether metrics are improving. It is easily understood by the employees.

Implementation of the VPM boards requires management and leadership commitment to provide the required supports, such as a clear SOP with support structure for the technician's response time to a machine down, area leader's support system to resolve any material supply issues and supervisors, and support to ensure problem solving is completed quickly.

The leadership team's commitment must be visually seen by the employees because this drives the employee's commitment and passion to achieve better performance and generate ideas for CIs. When a problem is not resolved quickly, the management team must ensure the technical team is involved to resolve it and ensure the same problems do not repeat again. Problem solving and problem prevention must be taken very seriously by everyone at all levels in the organisation.

Toyota Production System (TPS)

TPS is a living system. It is not a toolkit or a roadmap but a culture of how we live it. You must live it to understand it, and it continuously evolves. I have seen many companies that find it overwhelmingly seductive to have a toolkit and a roadmap. Because of this desire, lean consulting companies feed on this need and happily provide their customers with what these companies want.

The common mistakes companies make when learning the Toyota culture of lean include the following:

- Giving this journey a name like lean or Six Sigma or making it a programme.
- Using a roadmap to show the way to achieve lean.

- Senior leaders not directly involved, assigning the middle management team to deploy this as a programme.
- The companies fail to see that this is a cultural transformation journey. It is a relentless CI, a lifetime with no finishing point.
- Senior leaders do not take responsibility for leading this cultural change. This is a difficult journey that requires leaders commitment.
- A lean manager assigned to deploy the lean journey (thinking it is programme) is not acceptable. This is not a one-person job, but it is an organisation's people transformation journey. A lean manager should assist in toolkit and capability training, namely kanban, 5S, problem solving, and SMED and track the improvements of lead-time reduction, inventory reduction, changeover time reduction, product cost reduction, throughput improvements, and visual factory (and visual performance). They should organise the weekly updates with the leadership team.

This culture needs the top leader of the company to fundamentally build a new culture, engage into deeply understanding the people and the processes, and focus first and foremost on satisfying the customers. As we progress through the lean journey, companies are maturing from process-improvement toolkits to lean value stream management, employee engagement in daily problem solving, and self-aware leadership aligned to the right business problems. This means to live a business transformation that puts customers first and does this through developing people culture and capabilities. Employees who are doing the work are constantly improving the work and make the problems visible, helping them to think about how to solve these problems. There are tools, whether it is kanban, 5S, SOP, to establish a standard and to make any deviations from the standard visible to the employees in the workgroup. Then, the workgroup develops the problem-solving skills to identify the root cause and solve the real problem.

If these tools do not change the way people work and think about their own processes, the tools are a failure. If the leaders and managerial team do not understand how to use the tools to unleash the creativity and motivation of their people, then they are not true leaders but are just administrators of a bureaucratic system.

TPS is the company's pursuit of operational excellence, which is called the 4P Model. This drives the intense focus and everyone's energy, from senior management down to the operators in the shop floor, to constantly find a better way and remove waste in the process and in their daily work.

The culture of respect for people and CI resides as an organisational culture. Everyone in the organisation must have the external focus on adding value to the customers and shareholders.

Toyota's 4P Model

1. Philosophy

This is the foundation to base the management decisions on long-term philosophy even at the expense of short-term financial goals.

2. Process

It should constantly be focused on improving and eliminating waste, creating flow, and removing the 3M wastes.

3. People (and Partners)

In respect to people, constantly challenge them for better performance and grow their capability, creativity, and ability to always find better ways. Challenge your employees with creative spirit and encourage them to realise the goals or dreams (without losing the employees drive) and constantly maintain high energy.

4. Problem Solving

Create the culture to continuously improve and learn. Train all the employees to use the A3 methodology to solve problems daily and implement preventive actions to ensure the problems do not recur. The people make all the difference in the organisation.

The Three Enemies of Lean

There is a reason why the muda is there, and the reason often has something to do with the other two enemies of lean: muri and mura. This means the three enemies of lean are interrelated and should be considered simultaneously in a never-ending quest to improve and to achieve manufacturing excellence.

Lean Agile Manufacturing Systems and Culture

As shown in the preceding sections, lean manufacturing is crucial to the deployment of integrated process efficiency in mass customisation. However, the introduction of lean manufacturing itself needs a reassessment of the organisational culture. This is because waste reduction often requires the emergence of a new work culture. Instead of pushing as much work as possible out to the shop floor, the emphasis shifts to how materials have to be pulled to the line when production requires them.

The change to a lean manufacturing culture is a profound one. Attempts to introduce new cultures trigger powerful organisational defence routines that undermine the new culture. This ultimately stifles the transition of the lean process from the cell and shop-floor stage to the value stream and value systems stage, which is necessary for mass customisation.

It has been argued that while JIT is associated with basic techniques of inventory and production control, and TQM is a set of basic techniques that reduces process variance, HRM is a set of practices that shape the organisational environment in which the basic techniques are implemented.

There is a similar finding that provided an indication of the close relationship between JIT and people. The finding shows that the relationship between the use of JIT practices and manufacturing performance was not significant. However, there was a very strong relationship between JIT practices and infrastructure practices, which included quality management, workforce management, manufacturing strategy, organisational characteristics, and product design.

The necessity to focus on people issues extends beyond lean manufacturing and mass customisation. It extends to organisational attempts to enhance the level of agility in manufacturing. Several agility providers (practices, methods, tools, and techniques facilitating a capability for agility) also showed evidence of the need to look at people issues. Through a survey that involved 1,000 companies and based on a total of 12 case studies (Zhang and Sharifi, 2000), they concluded that practices related to people and organisational issues are both important to manufacturers and highly effective in enhancing levels of agility in the organisation.

Despite the apparent importance of taking cultural imperatives into consideration when attempting to increase levels of mass customisation, there has been little or no focus on issues that attempt to integrate the key dimensions of agile manufacturing systems. These dimensions relate to strategies, technology, people, and systems. In a similar vein, there is a dearth of empirical evidence regarding the operational characteristics related to agile manufacturing.

There are key concerns related to a predominantly technology-focused approach in the adoption of agile manufacturing strategies. There is an argument that it is necessary to have the right combination of strategies, culture, business practices, and technology for agile manufacturing.

The human factors play a significant role in the implementation of agile manufacturing. The relatively high emphasis placed on strategy, technology, and systems and less emphasis on people as evidenced by the number of articles in the literature seems to downplay the importance of HR management in the context of new work or organisational culture.

Concept of Organisational Culture

Culture represents how an organisation learns to adapt over time. It comprises common values that have been inherited and assumptions used over time by the organisation's members to analyse both their behaviour and that of others. It is the glue that holds an organisation together, and it is socially constructed.

It takes a strategic leadership commitment to transform a culture to one that promotes competitiveness. Likewise, the leadership team's communication and commitment to implement lean manufacturing is indicative of the management's commitment.

An essential feature of an agile organisation is that its members should be regarded as partners when implementing lean and agile manufacturing that enables the transition to be successful to deliver the intended results. This highlights the importance of innovative practices that enable organisations to exhibit high levels of adaptability, which is required to meet the changing customer requirements.

Cultural Dimensions

There are four dimensions to an organisation culture. They include the following:

- Mission and vision
- Adaptability
- Involvement
- Consistency

This section attempts to show how these dimensions manifest as attempts to operationalise lean agility are made.

Denison (1990) defines cultural stability as the property of having high levels of agreement, consistency, and unity of purpose. Cultural flexibility is the property of having high-involvement and adaptable work practices. Consistency and mission are oriented towards cultural stability whereas involvement and adaptability emphasise an organisation's capacity for cultural flexibility and change.

Larger and more functionally organised manufacturing enterprises had to be oriented towards stability for them to engage in mass production. However, as organisations began to engage in mass customisation, they had to become increasingly oriented towards a higher level of flexibility and agility and adopt a lean approach to manufacturing (Pine, 1993). This appears to suggest that from a cultural perspective, a shift towards cultural and organisational leadership flexibility is required for mass customisation.

People Involvement and Empowerment

People involvement and empowerment are critical for the factories of the future implementing the smart manufacturing and achieving the high-performing employee work culture. Organisations with high-involvement cultures have individuals that are empowered, whose capabilities are continually developed and who work in a team-oriented setting. This kind of culture is an important requirement for organisations that seek to enhance their level of mass customisation since the mass customisation process is dependent on how well an organisation can transform its leadership role towards adopting a more empowering workstyle. Having a high-involvement culture is also a prerequisite to information sharing and developing trust amongst employees, which is another key requirement for mass customisation (manufacturing transition) as evidenced by a study carried out by Liao et al. (2011). The progress experienced is synonymous to the employees' efforts and endeavour in any organisation, and this is possible with the dynamic involvement of those employees at the workplace.

The enhancement of agility through an increasing focus on improving employee involvement has been documented extensively in the literature. This suggests that unless the level of employee involvement is increased, the agility required to engage in mass customisation will be somewhat constrained.

The job function involvement model below summarises the investment of time and resources of the management functions to maintain the current established SOP and to improve the current system for the better. Sustaining the current SOP is important, and this will ensure all expected results (lead time, quality, and cost). Improving the current work processes, new ideas, and breakthrough results will be the core responsibility of the top leadership and the middle management team. This does not mean that the lower functional groups are not involved. They will be, but the leadership and managerial team must see to it they take the total accountability and be personally involved to ensure that the various functional teams are delivering better results and performance continuously—the concept of every day a better day.

Figure 14: Job Function Involvement Model

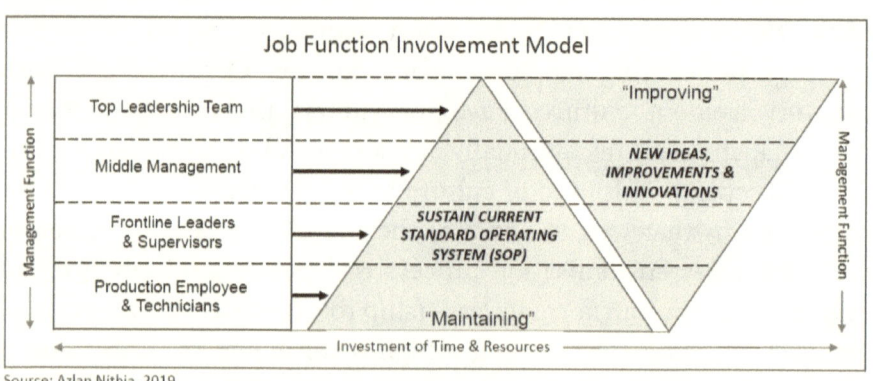

Source: Azlan Nithia, 2019

The maintenance of the current SOP must be adhered by the employees and the technicians who are involved in the daily production execution. This is their core job function that is expected of them all the time to ensure smooth running of the daily operations and keep the production running per the quality and throughput targets. This group of employees will also participate in daily improvement activities and the small group activities, but their main function is to maintain and sustain the current SOP at the workplace.

The front-line leaders and supervisors have an important role to ensure the employees are maintaining the current SOPs and delivering results against all the expected targets and goals. This functional group must ensure that the visual performance boards are updated on a timely manner, and the safety procedures and the 5S systems are well managed. They will participate in the daily gemba kaizen activities (daily improvement) to ensure all equipment, machines, material flow, required resources, headcount, and technician support are available at the right time at the right quantities. Problem solving will be this group's daily routine work; therefore, they are required to constantly find the 3M wastes in the system and then to reduce and eliminate them. This requires a structured and simple problem-solving kaizen methodology that can be used by everyone in the organisation. The middle management's role is to give support and help and provide required skills trainings for the front-line leaders and the supervisors to achieve their goals.

CHAPTER 5

Smart Manufacturing: Factory of the Future

The Inevitable Manufacturing Transition

This transition is to reimagine the manufacturing industry to achieve global competitiveness by the successful adoption of greater digital technology of a connected factory to increase efficiency, speed, and agility. The industries require the ability to be able to rapidly transition into the new smart manufacturing paradigm and be able to respond to the demanding market changes quickly in a digitally connected marketplace to sustain higher levels of customer competitiveness.

With the advent of smart manufacturing and the factory of the future, there is an urgent need for all industries and organisations to transform their manufacturing operations and supply chain. It also requires a learning organizational culture to successfully implement the requirements of the factory of the future. This transition will better position the industry to improve the customer responsiveness and to become a globally competitive supplier. This transition will require a strong lean manufacturing foundation. The lean foundation will facilitate the implementation of smart manufacturing, connected factory and IoT. This enables the organization to achieve continuous growth of business competitiveness and improve the company's profitability.

The digital, cyber technologies and smart manufacturing must be the forefront of all the manufacturing industries. The industry will continue to be influenced by the industrial revolution's technological advancements in discrete and process manufacturing, supply chain, marketing, and consumer interface. The industries have already experienced over the decades various industry revolutions since the first invention of mechanised machines, followed by conveyor system production, mass production, and emergence of the digital technologies that started challenging and changing the manufacturing platforms rapidly. The manufacturing is already evolving into a sophisticated cyber system with connected end-to-end supply chain (or value chain), application of industrial IoT, and connected intelligence in manufacturing, production, logistic, and related industries.

The industrial revolution 4.0 was initially conceived in 2015 in the context of manufacturing application, but this has fast expanded to all industries around the globe. The discussion of industrial revolution 5.0 has already started in 2018. The duration between the industrial revolutions is also getting shorter and shorter, such as between first and second revolutions as compared to third and fourth revolutions. The industrial revolution 5.0 is already concurrently happening with the fourth revolution. The future industrial revolutions will continue to develop in parallel and concurrently with a lot shorter durations.

To understand the benefit and impact of the industrial rapid transition into smart manufacturing, it is essential to see the full value chain, which must include suppliers of the materials and components needed for your internal manufacturing processes, the connected end-to-end digital supply chain, and the final destination, which is digitally connected to the end consumer.

Personalising product, producing mixed models, increasing variety, and responding quickly to consumer demands are some of the goals that can only be achieved with the connected customer-centric smart factory of the future. These industries must respond with increasing sense of demanding customers who only value speed, cost, agility, and innovative VA services.

In the end, all industries will remain as business but as a smart-connected business in a digitally connected world. These smart businesses will have the innovative twist of innovation and transformational digital technologies of business models and processes that will increase profit, decrease product costs, enhance the consumer experience, optimise consumer loyalty through the lifetime value, and increase global market with innovative growth, but still remain relevant and responsive to any market digital disruption.

In an industrial revolution in a digitally matured technological ecosystem, we will always find new disruptions, new advancements, new capabilities with quantum leaps. This kinds of changes in a digitally connected world will be happening quicker than ever.

Steps to Become Factory of the Future

The investment required to implement the technologies, automation, robots, and connected factory is high. It is extremely important for the company to ensure it has assessed its gaps and upgraded its foundation so that it can successfully implement the advanced technologies. The investment of advanced technologies is to further help the company achieve higher level of customer responsiveness and deliver products faster and at a lower cost. The end in mind must be very clear, and the investments must be strategically connected to the final expected results.

Figure 15: Steps to Become Factory of the Future (AURI Model)

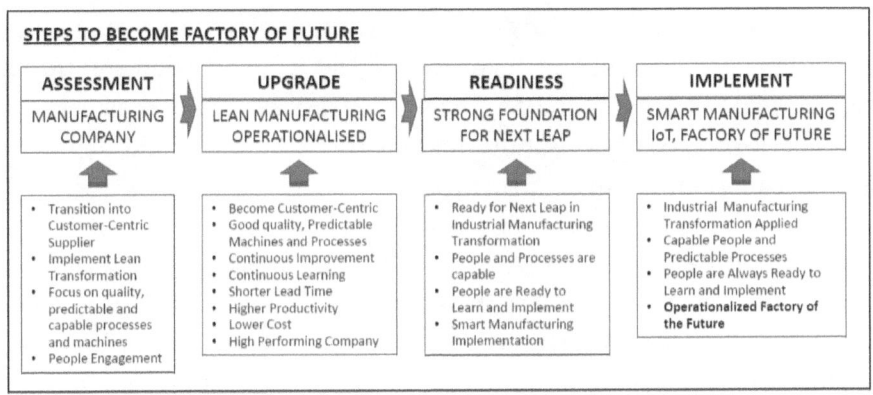

Source: Azlan Nithia, 2019

There are four critical steps (or the AURI model) required for any company to step up its technological capabilities to become a digitally connected factory of the future with a connected world-class supply chain system. The AURI model stands for assessment, upgrade, readiness, and implement.

Step 1: Assessment

This is the important first step to discover the current stage of the company and its manufacturing excellence gaps. This assessment is key to establishing the amount of work required in both the manufacturing processes and the people readiness gap.

The people assessment will take into consideration the ability of the people in the organisation currently to be able to adopt to new technologies, capability to continuously learn new ideas, and ability to be able to implement new technologies. This will also require an agile organisation that is able to adapt to changes, which includes the leaders of the company.

Step 2: Upgrade

Based on the assessment study of the current stage, it requires upgrading the company (capability of the processes and its people culture) into a readiness stage—that is, to be a customer-responsive, customer-centric, high-performance organisation that has fully embraced and deployed all the lean manufacturing principles.

A lean organisation is an organisation that has operationalised capable and predictable processes and machines (with good OEE) producing good quality, demonstrating high productivity, and yet continuously improving them further to make it even better and better—a relentless journey. To achieve a high level of manufacturing processes and machine efficiency, it requires employees who can make it happen.

The employees must be good at solving problems, continuously improve the manufacturing processes, relentlessly identify NVA activities, and remove them. Daily improvement is the people culture. The upgrade is important to succeed.

If the manufacturing processes or the people or both have not reached the acceptable level of readiness, it is important to bridge this readiness gap first through the process and people upgrade using lean methodologies. It is pointless to connect a bunch of poor-performing machines to a central monitoring system and not have capable employees to solve the problems rapidly. This will only cripple the company because it is not ready to embrace the higher levels of advanced technologies. It will result in wasted capital investments and may even negatively impact its business.

Therefore, to have capable machines and capable employees is the prerequisite to embark into smart manufacturing, the connected factory of the future. Once the organisation has implemented a strong lean manufacturing foundation, it is ready to upgrade its manufacturing processes and its supply chain system with smart manufacturing technologies.

Step 3: Readiness

This is the step closer to becoming the factory of the future. Step 3, readiness, is about ensuring all the operational ecosystems are ready for the organisation. This step will ensure that the investment dollars are strategically invested in the right advanced digital technologies, automation, and IoT. At this readiness stage, all the processes and machines are already upgraded to a predictable and capable level to produce good-quality parts all the time efficiently. The people are engaged in daily continuous-improvement activities, continuously learning new things to apply, solving problems daily, and applying good 5S.

It is very important to ensure the investment and the types of digital and automation technologies will improve the company's customer responsiveness, reduce delivery lead time, lower product cost, and position the company to a sustainable growth path and become a globally competitive company. If it does not deliver those benefits, then the return on investment (ROI) may not be achieved as planned.

Step 4: Implement

The implementation stage, step 4, is where high-capital investments will be made to deploy the implementation of smart manufacturing technologies, automation, robotics, IoT, and connected factory of the future. The company must rethink its business model and supply chain systems in the new digitally connected ecosystem.

This new system will deliver a better customer responsiveness with digitally connected platforms and productivity increases with the implementation of connected factory systems. The lead time declines due to intelligent monitoring and alert systems that trigger quick response to solve problems, better process quality with digital and visual monitoring systems, increased machine utilisation with factory monitoring, and rapid response time. The transition towards co-creation of products will deliver shorter time to market, better data-driven value (end-to-end) and human-robot collaboration. These will result in better customer responsiveness, good return on capital investments and increase the market share.

There must be a clear vision and objective connected to the new business model that will be driven by higher levels of customer responsiveness and organisational agility. Implementing smart manufacturing is not about spending capital investment to catch the trends of industrial revolution, to show robots in action, or to look elegant. Smart manufacturing is about delivering sustainable better business results and to be able to compete globally, respond faster, responsive supply chain more quickly, and lower cost.

Transitioning to Factory of the Future

The figure below explains the process of transitioning from current state to the factory of the future. The current state of the company must be strengthened with the lean manufacturing implementation to create the lean organisational culture.

Figure 16: Lean and Smart Manufacturing—Transitioning to Factory of the Future

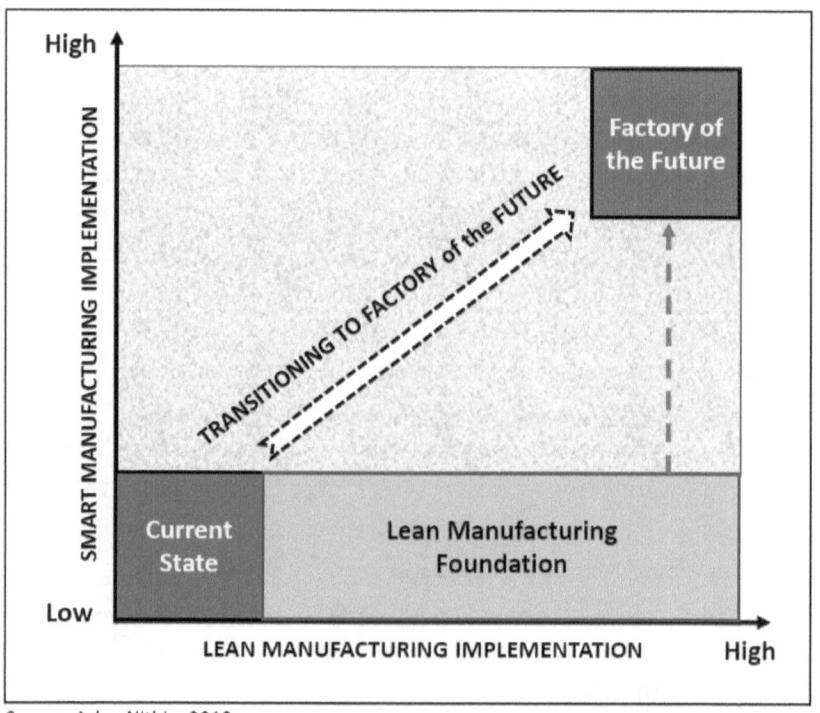

Source: Azlan Nithia, 2019

The key principles of lean are to continuously improve the process efficiency, predictable machines, customer responsiveness, problem-solving, eliminate NVA activities; continuously reduce cost; and be agile. These are important foundations required for any company to succeed in manufacturing or business; it is the readiness prerequisite required to apply smart manufacturing and, in parallel, continuously strengthen the lean manufacturing implementation.

The organisation must also periodically complete the VSM to identify opportunities to improve, eliminate NVA activities, improve the value within the company, and increase the value for the customer.

Lean Manufacturing + Smart Manufacturing = Factory of the Future

The organisation that applies lean manufacturing dynamics will continue to thrive by sustaining strong profitability, growth, and innovation even though unpredictability is the norm and change is constant. The lean's strong customer focus and customer responsiveness is key for any business survival in any industry and company. When the company had already developed a strong customer-focused lean manufacturing culture, then implementing smart manufacturing becomes a logical next step to increase the value chain and to take the company to higher levels of customer responsiveness.

Smart Manufacturing and Market Competitiveness

The figure below explains the three types of smart manufacturing implementation scenarios and how these scenarios will have an impact in the organisation's market competitiveness, customer responsiveness, and market share.

1. Scenario 1 (Line A)

It refers to smart manufacturing implementation with automation, IoT, robotics, and a connected factory. The increase in the level of smart manufacturing implementation had correspondingly increased the market competitiveness. This will enable the company to achieve higher customer responsiveness, market share increase, and good return on capital investment. This is possible by having a strong lean manufacturing foundation in place, operationalising the customer-centric business focus; and then the company is ready for implementing the smart manufacturing. This is the prerequisite for smart manufacturing implementation readiness.

Figure 17: Smart Manufacturing Implementation versus Market Competitiveness

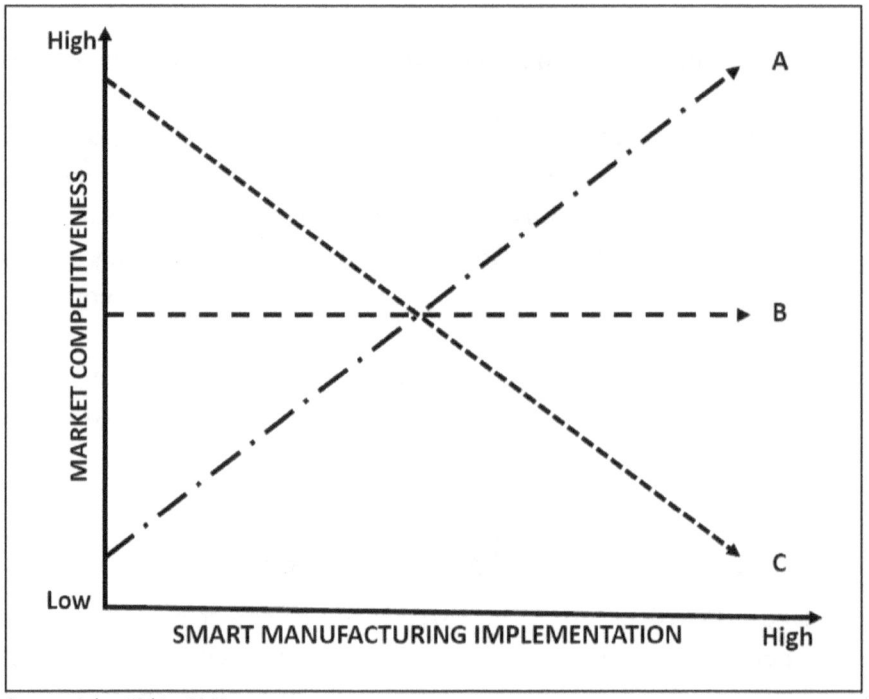

Source: Azlan Nithia, 2019

1. Scenario 2 (Line B)

Smart manufacturing is applied and completed. The increase in the level of smart manufacturing implementation did not increase the market competitiveness. The customer responsiveness did not increase and remained the same. Therefore, the market competitiveness and market share will remain the same. This condition is not a desired business condition because smart manufacturing is highly capital intensive; and ultimately, the investment cost will impact the product cost negatively. Therefore, ROI is important. This scenario 2 is also an indication of lack of lean manufacturing implementation. It should be creativity first (reduce NVA activities and simplify processes) before spending money on capital expenses. Any capital investment must increase the value for the company. The most important value is to increase customer responsiveness (by achieving faster delivery and lower cost).

2. Scenario 3 (Line 3)

Smart manufacturing is applied and completed. The increase in the level of smart manufacturing implementation decreased the market competitiveness. This is a common manufacturing trap for organisations embarking into the implementation of robotics and automation. This is the situation whereby the capital is invested prior to creativity. The creativity is driven by the lean manufacturing principles. Lean requires a careful study of every capital investment related to automation and robotics. It must improve customer responsiveness, increase the market share, reduce the lead time, and lower product cost. If these lean principles are ignored in the smart manufacturing implementation, then the manufacturing operation becomes less flexible. It can increase model changeover time; and this directly impacts the throughput, lead time, and product cost. This may quickly drive the company out of business.

The above three different scenarios indicate the importance of organisational readiness before implementing the smart manufacturing. Factory of the future are factories that have successfully operationalised lean manufacturing with strong people culture and efficient manufacturing processes. It refers to anything that an organisation invests in, especially one that involves automation, robotics, IoT, and capital investments. The ultimate goal is to increase customer responsiveness by increasing flexibility, agility, delivery lead time; lowering cost; and improving quality.

To compete successfully in the global market means to compete to win in the fierce customer-centric business. It is important that the organisational readiness assessment is achieved as explained in the 'Steps to Become Factory of Future (AURI Model)'.

The Industrial Revolution

In the last two hundred years, we have seen quantum leaps in technological innovations, continuous advancement of technology, and industrialisation. Between mid-1700s and early 1900s, there were many major inventions that can be classified as industrial revolutions 1.0 and 2.0 (IR 1.0 and IR 2.0). These two industrial revolutions created many inventions that were the basic and foundational needs for people, like the trains, steam engine ships, cars, planes, telephones, electric bulbs, radios, and tube televisions. Then followed by the industrial revolutions 3.0 and 4.0, which occurred in late 1900s and into 2000s. This was the era of digital and advanced technology, like the fax machines, mobile phones, internet, Wi-Fi, computers, electronic calculators, electric trains, high-speed trains, faster planes, digital televisions, high-performance semiconductors, programmable logic controllers, computer-controlled machines, Google search engines, Facebook, WhatsApp, and many more. This resulted in connecting the world and people digitally and quickly. This made the world a smaller place, and the connected digital global trade was advanced very rapidly.

The industrial revolution 4.0, which started in the early 2000s, we realised the advanced technologies that was developed to connect the machines for real time data collection and people working with machines collaboratively. The advanced robots that could be operated from remote locations, thousands of kilometres away. The IoT that connected the consumers with product designers and the manufacturers that allowed the real time information sharing on a common platform. These advancements reduced the product lead time to the market.

The generations of the industrial revolution can be briefly explained as below:

1. Industrial Revolution 1.0

It is the era of mechanical systems and systems that used steam to power engines and other mechanical movements. This was also when the mechanical loom was invented and later the factories to manufacture cloth. This had further stimulated cotton and textile industry. This was the beginning of the first Industrial Revolution.

2. Industrial Revolution 2.0

There were many industrial innovations and inventions that changed the industry rapidly. There's advancement in electricity production and supply, mass-production systems, conveyors and belts run by electric motors, faster trains, telephones, motorcycles, cars, airplanes, steam power ships, televisions, and many more. Numerous mechanically automated machines were used in the manufacturing industries to achieve higher levels of productivity outputs with better quality, and other industries like farming and construction started using many types of mechanically operated equipment to increase their output and to lower the cost. The Ford Model T was introduced in 1913. It rolled out of Ford factory's assembly lines and marked the beginning of high-volume mass production. These industrial developments continued to evolve and progressed rapidly throughout the world; and later, mechanical automations were used to further increase production outputs, improve quality, and reduce cost.

3. Industrial Revolution 3.0

It refers to the application of computers, IT systems, electronic, high-performance semiconductors, programmable logic controllers, multi-function IC chips (dual-core chips), high-performance micro-sized microprocessors, advancement in mobile phones, Facebook, Google search engines, digital libraries, WhatsApp, WeChat, internet banking, wireless technology. Mobile networks became faster from 1G to 4G (fourth-generation mobile network). It is also the application of advanced automation to reduce lead time and improve quality. Customer responsiveness became a key competitive advantage. It also introduced robots in manufacturing, fibre optics, high-speed electric trains, electric cars, and many more.

The globalisation of businesses, advanced digital supply chain systems, and internet marketing changed the way we forecast customer requirements, manufacture products, and market products and services. These advancements and high-tech industrialisations had made the world a small place. Marketing products digitally and globally had evolved almost every industry around the world.

4. Industrial Revolution 4.0

The continuation of industrial revolution 3.0 successes evolved further into industrial revolution 4.0. The convergence towards the digital cyber systems started creating numerous digital and intelligent technological innovations disrupting the manufacturing value chain. The operational excellence leveraged disruptive technologies to develop new business models, advanced analytics, additive manufacturing (3D printing), advanced robotics, industrial IoT, and digitally connected factory. It presented the immense opportunity of intelligent processes and systems to achieve better quality, higher efficiency, increased speed to market, product co-creation, increased customer responsiveness, flexibility, and responsive production system.

The industrial revolution 4.0 has made all industries scrambling to understand what the digital cyber systems and advanced automation can do for them and how these will change their company's competitiveness in the marketplace. It became overwhelming for many businesses to invest in the capital expenses required to implement digital connectivity, IoT, robotics, and automation. It is a critical point of decision for the industry. Either the organisation transforms and embraces it, or it fails to adopt the digital connected factory and gets eliminated.

It requires the full implementation of smart manufacturing technologies that fully adopt automation, human-machine interface, and full traceability from customer order to delivery. There is an urgency to understand that the cost of manual labour will continue to rise but the cost of automation will continue to go down.

The development to upgrade the 4G mobile digital network became urgent as the remote robots are required to operate with extremely high precision and accurately perform the various activities in real-time on various jobs from a remote station that could be located hundreds or thousands of kilometres away. The emergence of 5G digital network that operates up to 50 to 100 times faster than 4G is critical to successfully implement functions like using remote robots to perform an open-heart or even brain surgeries remotely without human surgeons and many other kinds of sophisticated remote-controlled equipment.

This fourth revolution had reset people readiness backwards, especially on how ready they are to learn fast, adopt, and implement new digital technologies flawlessly. The teaching methods and the subjects taught in the schools, colleges, and universities had to be revised to include the advanced digital technologies, robotics, industrial IoT, and many other related subjects. It requires high level of people's ability to continuously learn new methods, adapt quickly to changes, respond to customers quickly, work on multiple processes, and respond to real-time digital data.

In a nutshell, the concept of industrial revolution 4.0 encapsulates the development of the manufacturing sector from a laborious mass-production model to an integrated, seamless automated connected factory, the factory of the future, and digitally connected end-to-end supply chain system from consumer order to delivery. There is a greater need for more diverse and complex skillsets to improve productivity in high-mix low-quota (volume) production environments. The market developments and consumer preferences will push companies to develop more innovative solutions to meet evolving demands of the consumer needs.

5. Industrial Revolution 5.0

This fifth revolution is the new era of modern manufacturing, and collaborative robots will be the forefront of this revolution. There will be a greater application of human-robot collaboration (with infinite possibilities) in manufacturing processes and many other industries including the deskilling of the medical industry. The co-creation of products with customers with customer obsession, mass customisation, agility (people and processes), and customer experience will become a norm for every industry. The smart manufacturing application in the manufacturing industries will be a norm and a prerequisite for competing in a digitally connected marketplace while achieving zero-waste production. A much more advanced human-machine connected interface system will continue to be developed and applied in many different industries.

The high-quality 3D printing will be the industrial production reality, especially with the various advancements in material sciences and special material technology. The additive manufacturing processes will eliminate the time-consuming manufacturing processes. The medical industry will benefit from the advancement of additive 3D printing. The 3D printing technology for producing very fine precision reconstructive bones will enable the reconstruction of very complex bone contours and uses super lightweight materials. There are many more applications in the medical industry.

The new product introduction process, from product ideation to product available in the market lead time, will be extremely short with the application of the additive 3D printing. It will eliminate all the manufacturing processes, tooling, and equipment. The time to produce the product will be equal to the time to print the parts. The high-speed 3D printers will print a variety of different parts when required with high precision, high quality, and lower cost. This will change the landscape of manufacturing industry globally.

The 5G digital network that operates 50 to 100 times faster than 4G will be further enhanced to an even faster digital connectivity. This will increase the remote human-like robots used to perform surgeries in the global medical industry. This will reduce the need for highly skilled surgeons because these human-like remote robots can perform surgeries very precisely and work continuously for twenty-four hours every day.

This advanced digital network technology will be used to even remotely navigate airplanes, cars, drones, and self-driving vehicles.

The industrial revolution will continue to evolve and improve digital connectivity and advanced technologies by creating a seamless global market competition and complete transparency of every single activity happening around the industrial world, especially the consumers' preference or demand pattern. It will require a strong organisational agility and people-learning fitness to be able to continuously learn, adopt, and implement newer industrial digital advancements rapidly as and when it becomes available. The speed of adoption does matter and will matter on flawless quick implementation to capture and apply the new business competitive advantage to sustain the continuous profitability of the company. Every time a new technology is adopted, it must create a new value for the organisation, and the value chain must be connected to increasing the customer responsiveness as the end goal.

The future of the industry is about the survival of the fittest. The fittest are those organisations that are quick to learn and quick to implement new technologies flawlessly to strengthen and grow the business rapidly and globally. Organisations must compete like a fish in the ocean (globally) and not like a fish in pond (domestic).

Conclusion

The new industrial revolution in manufacturing is focused in achieving smart manufacturing and the factories of the future. To achieve this, it requires the implementation of a connected factory to become a reality. The machines, robots and the manufacturing processes will deliver real-time data, comprehensive analysis and will monitor performance and efficiencies.

To reimagine the manufacturing industry by successful adoption of greater digital technologies to increase efficiency, speed, and agility, the manufacturing industry requires the ability to be able to rapidly transition into the smart manufacturing paradigm by adopting the latest technologies. This will give the companies the ability to quickly respond to the demanding market changes and customer responsiveness in a digitally connected marketplace. This can only be achieved by implementing higher levels of manufacturing competitiveness.

The manufacturing industry is constantly evolving from the use of intensive labour force to the use of automation and robotics to increase production efficiency, reduce lead time, and reduce the cost of products. An efficient manufacturing sector would pave the way to enhance the industry's productivity and required to be supported with high-skilled talent pool, innovation, continuous learning capacity, and support for the well-being of the country's national economic prosperity.

Manufacturing Industry Challenges

The manufacturing industries are constantly confronted with serious issues of rising labour cost, lack of skilled talents who can adopt and implement latest technologies rapidly, high capital investment, globally challenging business environment, and increasingly demanding customer requirements. The manufacturing industries must be capable to constantly evolve and transform by adopting and applying latest efficient technologies to meet the changing and challenging customer requirements. The ability to quickly transition and transform to deliver shorter lead times, better qualities, and lower cost will decide whether the organisation will survive or gets eliminated.

As manufacturing companies look into their next decade of growth and business sustainability, they must rethink the way they are doing their business currently. Only through implementing higher technology manufacturing methods, reinventing, innovating the systems, and running intelligent smart operations can they stay relevant and continue to be highly competitive in the global business environment.

The organisations must continuously focus to improve and strengthen their lean manufacturing foundations (both in people and process) and continuous learning culture so that smart manufacturing applications can bring in the required customer responsiveness and organisation and people readiness to succeed in achieving the factory of the future status. The organisation's relentless journey to remove NVA activities by applying and eliminating the 3M wastes (muda, mura, and muri) are basic requirements to improve productivity and reduce lead time and cost.

People Talent Challenges

Transitioning to the new smart manufacturing paradigm is driven by two key pillars: the people readiness and the manufacturing process readiness. Both people and process excellence will deliver operational excellence. The people readiness is a priority because only capable people with relevant skill and knowledge will adopt and implement efficient processes. Developing the required human capital and retaining our existing talents by providing them with the right skill and technical support are critical.

The People Talent Requirements

- Talent and skills—able to continuously learn, adopt, and implement new technologies rapidly
- The people culture and readiness to adopt and manage processes in smart manufacturing environment
- Training needs for the new engineers and technicians to be able to maintain and improve smart manufacturing equipment and processes

Appendix 1

Kaizen Event to Deliver Breakthrough Results

Kaizen is a Japanese word from the word *kai* and *zen*, which means *change* and *better*. Together, it means to improve to make it better or simply stated as 'continuous improvement'. CI is extremely powerful when it is developed into an organisational people culture. Everyone in the organisation making improvements on a daily basis will elevate the manufacturing and operational productivity constantly, so today is better than yesterday. These month's results are better than last month's results; similarly, this year's results are better than last year's results.

When the continuous-improvement culture is imbedded as the company DNA, then the constant improvements will position the company as a competitive company with the capability to constantly improve and be better than the competition.

Being a lean organisation means the organisation is constantly focused on satisfying the customer and improving the customer responsiveness by continuously improving the process, removing waste in every process in the organisation from beginning (receiving orders), making the products, delivering the orders on time, and collecting the payment on time. By doing so, the organisation can continuously reduce lead time, improve productivity (throughput increases), and reduce cost.

These improvements will increase customer delights and customer satisfaction, and the customer will place more orders.

A kaizen event is normally a five-day event, and it consists of five important steps. Normally, it's one step a day. This is called the full kaizen event. The full kaizen event is also called the kaizen breakthrough event because in five days, the kaizen team implements a major breakthrough or improvements beyond 20%.

There are also smaller kaizen events. They are called the kaizen blitz. This event is for delivering quick results, and the durations are very short, between half day and two days.

The Lean Thinking Benefits

- Adds value to customers
- Creates flow in the manufacturing process
- Continuously improves and innovates
- Reduces lead time
- Treats people as an appreciating asset
- Applies kaizen for breakthrough results (improvements beyond 20%)

The kaizen breakthrough focuses on the following:

- Clear objectives, deliverables, and scope for the kaizen
- Bias for action and delivery of fast results
- Immediate results and new process functioning by day five
- Use of creativity to improve before spending the capital money
- Use of creativity to achieve immediate process improvement
- Focus on physical transformation
- Overcoming of resistance for change
- Team-based process
- Involvement of everyone in the kaizen team in the improvement
- Cross-functional team members
- Focus on rapid improvement, tight focus on Time
- Necessary resources made available immediately

Five-Step Kaizen Process

1. Step One (Day One): Train—Lean Methodology Training and Exercises

Step one is mostly about training the participants on lean principles: the 3M wastes (muda, mura, and muri); VA and NVA; one-piece flow; pull system; CI; management of daily improvements; SOPs; JIT; jidoka; respect for people; lead-time reduction; and principles of kaizen breakthrough results. The kaizen objectives and deliverables are discussed. Team leader and members are identified.

2. Step Two (Day Two): Discover—Analyse the Current Process or Work (Current State)

Team leaders and members are identified; objectives, deliverables, and scope are clearly explained. The team is at the shop floor or the area where the kaizen is taking place. It understands all the current processes, the SOPs, and how the work is being done. The team also identifies the wastes (opportunities), inventories, reworks, and one-piece-flow opportunities. The team also attempts hands-on improvements to test ideas.

The team meets to discuss the current processes and all the opportunities for improvements.

3. Step Three (Day Three): Doing—Make the Improvements

The team will complete the 5S activities and make the workplace and the process flow visual. Determine the material replenishment system, takt time, and customer requirements and make improvements. Implement all the improvement ideas and make corrections as required.

The team meets to discuss the outcome of the improvements done, as well as its results and refinements required.

Step Four (Day Four): Refinement—Refine and Improve to Achieve the Results

Establish the new SOP and then discuss with the employees affected in the area or the process and make further refinement. Install the kaizen newspaper (it could be flip chart) to track the hourly performance of the new method and continue to refine. Train all the affected individuals with the new change and the new SOP. Operate fully in the new system and track performance and any refinement done hourly.

The team meets to discuss the results and compares with the expected deliverables. It establishes the visual performance tracking boards and writes up the implementation of the new SOPs and new trainings required.

5. Step Five (Day Five): Presentation and Celebrate

Review all the key learnings and the new thirty-day action list (called the thirty-day kaizen action list). Any outstanding actions and improvements must be completed within thirty days. The team must also implement the MDI at the area/process that was under kaizen. There will be some refinements that may be required for the next several days or weeks. This will require daily review and refinement of the new SOPs, material movements, visual performance tracking (hourly tracking of target versus actual), and work methods.

Prepare the final presentation (usually in PowerPoint slides) and present it to the organisation's leadership team. The presentation must include the team members' names, objectives, deliverables, scope, current state discoveries, improvements made, future state implemented, improvements achieved (percentage of improvements and savings), thirty-day kaizen action list, MDI actions, and key learnings. The kaizen ends with the recognitions given to all the kaizen team members and a simple celebration of success.

Sustaining Kaizen Gains

- The thirty-day kaizen action list, homework requires part-time involvement by team leader and selected team members.
- Daily gemba walk by relevant employees and area heads and continuous MDI
- Train area leaders and operators.
  - Standard work, visual SOP
  - Visual controls and performance measurement (hourly and daily tracking)
  - Record countermeasures taken for any abnormality and problem resolution
- Post suggestion board (kaizen newspaper) in the work area and make sure that they are attended to daily during daily gemba walk (MDI).

Kaizen Rules

- Keep an open mind to change and be an equal-status team member.
- Maintain a positive attitude and listen to other members' ideas.
- Never leave in a silent disagreement. Speak up and participate.
- Create a blameless environment. Focus on moving forward.
- Practise mutual respect and do this every day.
- Treat others as you like to be treated.
- Every person can have a voice. There's no position or rank during kaizen activity.
- There's no such thing as a dumb question. Ask if you're not sure.
- Quick and simple is better than slow and elegant.
- Understand the improvement process and do it immediately.

Kaizen Business Strategy

- People are the most important appreciating asset in the company, and respect for people is critical. The well-trained people will develop efficient processes, continuously improve, and implement well-maintained machines.

- Reduce lead time and NVA activities in all processes relating to new product development, manufacturing processes, and administrative processes (from end to end).
- Use VSM to reduce or eliminate NVA activities, reduce inventory, and improve productivity. The 3M wastes (muda, mura, and muri) must be reduced and eliminated. Kaizen events are used to reduce and eliminate the 3M wastes. The mura and muri are various forms of constraints in the production processes and product flow.
- Continuously find and reduce/eliminate bottlenecks and constraints (muda) in the production process to constantly improve throughputs.
- Create the culture of 5S, which must be the core culture in every function in the organisation. Make it a requirement to make 5S score visual at every area and department.
- Visual performance tracking boards are critical, especially for engaging the people in that area. Tracking performance visually must include the target expected and actual achieved and show the variance (+ve or -ve). If it's below target, a brief comment must be written to explain the short fall. This must be installed and tracked every hour by every production line and process. There will be a large visual board in the shop floor to show the week's performance summary, all the various improvement activities, and problems solved in that week. This is the board that will be used during the weekly leadership meeting with the production people, and this is the meeting where the management and leadership team will offer any help (if required) to the team.
- Improve quality, cost, and delivery of the final product to the customer (OTIF).
- Establish a competitive advantage that will enable sales and profitability to continuously grow and sustain growth and profitability.
- Build an organisational culture where people involvement, engagement, and mutual respect encourage CI, continuous learning, problem solving, and innovation.

- Practice problem solving as a daily activity at every level. Problem-solving methodology must be made simple and easy for everyone to apply. Make problem solving as part of everyone's performance evaluation.
- Recognise small and big successes of every employee, celebrate good results, and appreciate every suggestion.

Appendix 2

Key Thoughts on Lean (The Lean Enterprise)

- Manufacturing processes are all about the *flow*, such as the flow of parts or products from one process to another process (raw material and information input up to the completion of the finished product or the final output).
- Business processes are also about the flow; but in business process, it is mostly the flow of knowledge.
- Problems are opportunities (like treasures newly found) for CIs.
- The problem is defined as the deviation from the standard, or the gap between the actual and the standard or the target.
- A sign of a problem is when the management team is making decisions without the current actual gemba data to support them.
- Tribal knowledge is *not* enough to make a smart decision. Knowledge may be a belief or someone's feeling or simply someone's hope. Go to the gemba. The truth is in the gemba.
- Kaizen event team members are generally from different functions. Sometimes people inside (or different functions) will give or make honest and candid assessments of the process or business case.
- The upstream is the supplier, and the downstream is the customer.

- Manufacturing is connected between the supplier (upstream) and customer (downstream); therefore, the whole system of supplier, manufacturing, and customer is the total value-driven supply chain (called the end-to-end value stream).
- Visual metrics are important for engaging the people to achieve a common goal.
- Measure performances that truly matter for the company. Make measurements visual. Every measurement must indicate the target versus the actual and state the reason for not achieving the target (if any).
- To successfully compete and sustain profitability, companies must focus on constantly eliminating waste from every manufacturing and business process.
- The foundation of a lean company is the deployment of a good 5S, visual flow, and VPM.
- Lean companies teach every employee in the organisation to be able to identify the 3M wastes (muda, mura, and muri) in everything they do.
- There are no shortcuts to manufacturing excellence. Achieving lean enterprise status requires senior leadership commitment and an organisational culture to drive it.
- Value is not about spending time on the job or showing up. It is about the accomplishment and the value created on the product.
- The first step to identify opportunities and wastes is to complete VSM from start to finish (end to end). Use the VSM outcome to identify all the opportunities and then use kaizen events to deep-dive and materialise the savings.

Companies must become a living business. Customers' needs will continuously evolve and shift. We must keep moving with them to ensure we stay relevant to our customers. Actively anticipate your customers' needs by living your business.

Appendix 3

Intimate Customer Knowledge to Grow the Business

When someone asks you a question, 'What does your company do?' what will be your answer? What will leaders and employees in your company answer? The answer will be 'We make PCBA, car components, computers, [and so on]'. All these kinds of services are replaceable by sourcing them from someone else. How do we position ourselves as irreplaceable? If your company has a 'makes products or provides services and makes parts and components' mentality, then you are limiting the company's ability to grow and to be customer-centric.

The organisation and the people must strongly believe and practise customer partnership, providing solutions and constantly increasing value for the customers. We depend on one another to be successful and to grow the business and market offerings. These kinds of relationship will require deep understanding of the customers and their challenges. There are inadequate processes and avenues for learning what the customers really need. One good example is the new product design. What are the features in the new product design that are truly important and matter for the customer? What features create the delight factors, and what are not valued by the customer? It is not about designing the product, but it is more about understanding customer.

- We must have similar visions and values like our customers to continually improve and grow with them and to become an integral part of our customers' success.
- The attitude and the thinking of our people in our organisation must be the customers are always right. Regularly ask for customer feedback and their complaints. Take these complaints very seriously and urgently. This is a golden opportunity to improve our products and services. Quickly resolve the complaints and show the customers the urgency and the speed you resolved their complaints. Ask for more feedback and be a solutions provider.
- Focus on long-term and be growth-oriented. Look for opportunities to move the customer-centric bar to customer partnership. Develop an intimate understanding of the customers' business, challenges, and needs and constantly commit to contribute to your customer's success. This is how a win-win strategy will grow you with the customers.
- There must be a Senior leadership commitment to spend time and be involved at the customer's place to understand the product, performance and opportunities to improve. This creates intimate customer knowledge with the sole purpose of understanding, learning, and improve, which drives innovative solutions and defines the value of your company. This will differentiate your company with other traditional companies.
- Practice does not make it perfect, but the right practice makes it perfect.
- Always carry out internal study (VSM) to evaluate the activities being done in the company by everyone in every function and ask questions like the following to trigger a kaizen blitz or kaizen event to eliminate any form of waste and increase value:

    o How does this activity add value for our customer?
    o Is the customer willing to pay for this activity?
    o How can we reduce inventories in every process?
    o How do we reduce lead time?

- What are the opportunities to reduce labour, material, and overhead cost?
- Does the senior leadership team understand all the above?

The lean approach to marketing is very different from the traditional approach to marketing. It starts with customer-centric questions and matches them with what you offer to your customers to meet their needs and wants and help solve their challenges. We must run a different race compared to our competitors, not running the same race but doing it faster, by entering areas your competitors are not ready to enter. To be a solution provider means you find the unique mix of products or services or activities that will create superior value for the customers. Examples are smaller lot sizes and with a high mix of products at a lower cost.

Appendix 4

Problem-Solving Case Study: A Case of the Porous Castings

As told by: Professor Dr Shrinivas Gondhalekar (aka Dr G)

The customer had finally agreed to the sampling procedure, but the tension persisted. Actually, the president of an auto ancillary manufacturer was never free from the fear of customer complaint. Just one complaint was enough. It could have serious ramifications not just for the company but also for the parent conglomerate. One fatal car crash, attributable to crankshaft failure, reported in the press would suffice to seal their fate. As auto ancillary manufacturer was the sole supplier of crankshafts, they could not even pass the buck to anyone else! The president knew exactly how Damocles must have felt about that sword.

The issue was porosity in the castings. Crankshafts were manufactured by pouring molten, ductile-grade iron into sand moulds. The resultant castings were machined and sent to the automobile company. The president knew that some of the castings displayed porosity deep inside. A porous crankshaft was weak and liable to break when the engine was running. Although the incidence of porosity was low, only one weak crankshaft was enough to cause an accident. In the emerging world of zero defects, liability for product failure was assuming alarming proportions. Claims ran into millions of dollars these days. And even if the company survived the financial blow, it could never hope to recover lost ground with the customer.

They had tried everything possible to correct the situation. They had even hired a consultant, who was an international foundry expert. He had suggested that they invest $5 million in changing the sand system. His calculations, based on overall operations of the entire foundry, revealed that they were using only 4kg of sand for every kilogram of metal cast, whereas for this particular casting technology, 6kg of sand were recommended. Insufficient sand in the mould allowed the liquid metal to cool and solidity too fast. It was well known in foundry technology that porosity was caused by differential rates of cooling within the casting. Metal has a propensity to shrink while solidifying, creating pockets of vacuum. Normally, molten metal from adjacent areas flows in to fill these gaps, resulting in a solid block of metal, which enjoys excellent strength. If, however, metal in the adjacent areas has already solidified, the gap created by the shrinking remains empty, thus creating what metallurgists call porosity.

There was another way porosity could occur: when molten metal is poured into the mould, it displaces the air in the mould. Mould designers provide paths, called vents, for the air to escape; but if these are inadequate, some air remains trapped inside, making the casting porous. Porous metal is spongy, lacks adequate strength, and permits oil and gases from one side to leak to the other. Good crankshafts are solid. They have no porosity.

The sand-system solution was far too expensive and would take nearly a year to implement as it involved rebuilding almost half the factory. Sand occupies a large volume of space and has to be transported to the mould-making area; once the castings solidify, it has to be broken away, cooled, and recycled. If you visit a foundry, you will find that the largest equipment visible usually pertains to sand silos and the sand-handling system.

But the company had no alternative. Consultations with other foundry experts had only confirmed that more sand was the solution. After many discussions with the chief executive officer of the conglomerate, it had been decided that the investment would be funded partly by the parent conglomerate group and partly by external borrowings. Inquiries had been floated, and negotiations were in progress to finalise the order.

Meanwhile, the quality control manager had come up with a countermeasure that would minimise the risk of delivering porous crankshafts to the customer. It consisted of determining which crankshaft had porosity by submitting each and every piece to an X-ray test. The technique was effective but also prohibitively expensive. The cost of castings had shot up by 30%, and the product was now making a negative contribution.

The president recalled, with a shudder, his attempt at negotiating prices upwards with the customer. The director of the auto company had been incredulous, asking him if he was aware that all vendors were only reducing prices in order to stay in business. In a suicidal moment, the president had threatened to stop making the castings if the price hike was not granted; but he was checkmated when the customer shrugged and said they would then withdraw all other products that were being sourced from the conglomerate. He had been coldly informed that a competing foundry had offered to set up dedicated operations in Thailand or India—an option that could always be considered. Beating a hasty retreat, he had managed to wrangle a small concession by touting the massive investment planned in order to improve quality. Instead of the X-ray testing, the customer had agreed to an inspection procedure, which would minimise the risk of faulty crankshafts being delivered. A sample of five crankshafts from the one hundred pieces that constituted a batch called a melt would be cut and examined in a destructive test. If none of them showed porosity, the entire batch could be dispatched to the customer. If one, two, or three of the samples showed porosity, then all the hundred would be X-rayed. The defective ones would be discarded, and only the good ones would be sent. However, if more than three samples showed porosity, the entire batch of one hundred would be discarded. This reduced the costs of doing X-rays somewhat, even though it left a finite risk. The customer had agreed with greatest reluctance.

The president knew they could not rest easy on the concession they had received. Unless this problem was rooted out, their business was in jeopardy. He knew had had to move fast.

He reached his office in a very disturbed state of mind that day; and when he saw that the quality control manager was waiting for him, he feared the worst. She was a large woman in her midforties, hawkish on the job, and unfamiliar with the art of diplomacy. The president hated her, but he also knew that he was still in his seat because she was preventing mishaps by sticking to her guns. Fearing that she had bad news, he waved her into his office and barked, 'All right, let me have it.'

She seemed faintly perplexed at this but spoke up nonetheless, 'I had been to a quality management seminar in Singapore yesterday. There was an expert from India who insisted that finding the root cause of quality-related problems did not need technical knowledge of the industry. It only needed application of hard deductive logic.'

'Okay.' The president was breathing again. Apparently, there had been no disaster. 'Well, get on with it. I don't have all day,' he said in the irascible manner he reserved for her.

'Well, I thought his approach was quite interesting. He demonstrated it with the help of case studies, where he had applied the method himself. He has done some extraordinary work in many countries across Asia. He has trained in Japan and has a great reverence for everything Japanese. I thought we could invite him to our company to attack the crankshaft problem. I checked out his credentials. He is brilliant and is quite well known in India, but he is also very expensive. I talked to him, explained our problem. He says we will recover the cost of his fees within two weeks.'

'If you think there is a reasonable chance of success, I am ready to risk it. You decide.'

The president was willing to explore any option that would save him precious time and money. The quality control manager was in her office, on the phone to India, before he could change his mind.

Dr G was scheduled to visit the auto ancillary company in early March. He thought this would be an interesting case for his ardent student, Payal. He asked her if she could join him on the visit. She was delighted at the opportunity, and they travelled together from Mumbai. On the plane, Payal was bubbling with enthusiasm. 'I hope you will be patient with me, sir,' she said. 'I am not a metallurgist, and neither am I an expert in techniques of problem solving. I shall be grateful, sir, if you would take me through the process step by step and explain the rationale at each stage.'

'Oh, I am not sure if it is a formal technique at all. I just use common sense and deductive logic. Maybe you can identify the steps since you will get a chance to see it as an outsider. I just do it on *automatic*.' She mulled over that for some time and then made notes in her little diary.

The next day, the quality control manager welcomed them warmly. She had taken an instant liking to this man in Singapore, and something about his distracted air had told her he was *the one*. 'It was like Morpheus finally meeting Neo,' she was to tell her colleagues later on.

After exchanging pleasantries with the problem-solving team, Dr G asked to be taken on a tour of the plant from the raw material receipt area to the finished product storage. 'It helps me to gain a perspective of the problem,' he told Payal. She observed that he brushed aside explanations of operating parameters but walked back and forth along the direction of the process flow, sometimes pausing to contemplate a machine in operation as if it were the *Mona Lisa*. The quality control manager watched his every move. When he had seen enough, he asked for a table to be set up near the shop floor. 'Now, please bring six to ten samples of your defective castings. Make sure they are recent samples, ideally, something produced today.'

Soon, six samples of porous castings, serially numbered, were placed on the table. Dr G picked up the first sample; and holding it up as if it were a newly acquired prize, he addressed the group. 'Look at this crankshaft. Does it have porosity?'

'Yes, it does,' they said.

'What other defect does it have?'

They stared at him blankly. Clicking his tongue impatiently, he said, 'Please look at the list of possible defects and find out which other defect is present in this very shaft.'

They could not make head or tail of it. The quality control manager was the first to comprehend. Pointing to a large board that displayed the quality parameters of the crankshaft in question, she asked, 'Are you referring to this? We check for hardness, sometimes the microstructure, perlite content, ferrite content, and the shape and spacing of the nodules. We check for blowholes, porosity or shrinkage, surface cracks, and cold shut.'

'What's a cold shut?' asked a bright voice. It was Payal. To her surprise, Dr G waved her query aside with a brusque 'Oh, never mind, I don't care what a cold shut is as long it is one of the defects.' Handing the crankshaft to the quality control manager, he said, 'Hold it in your hands. Now examine it, test it, and look up your test record. Do what you like, but tell me what other defect from your list is present in this particular sample.'

The whole group bent over the sample and started inspecting it. They declared that there was no cold shut, no surface crack, and no blowhole was visible; but they would need more time for chemical analysis of the metal.

'Let's start with the information that is readily available. If it suffices, well and good. If it does not, we will ask for more data.'

'Work with whatever data is available. Don't let incomplete data hold up the proceedings. You can always seek additional data as you go along,' Payal wrote in her small black diary. These notes would prove invaluable later on.

Other than porosity, there was nothing wrong with sample number 1. But sample number 2 had low hardness while sample 3 had a sand inclusion on the surface. The remaining samples had no defect, except porosity. Dr G was satisfied with the data. He did not need more samples.

'Porosity is not correlated with any other defect,' he whispered to his new associate. Down it went into her diary.

Picking up sample number 1 again, he asked, 'Where exactly is the porosity present in this sample? Also, please identify areas where porosity is completely absent.'

The sample was cut. Porosity was found at the junction of the flange and the shaft, in the area known as pin 1. Payal sketched the crankshaft in her diary. It is shown below in figure 3.1.

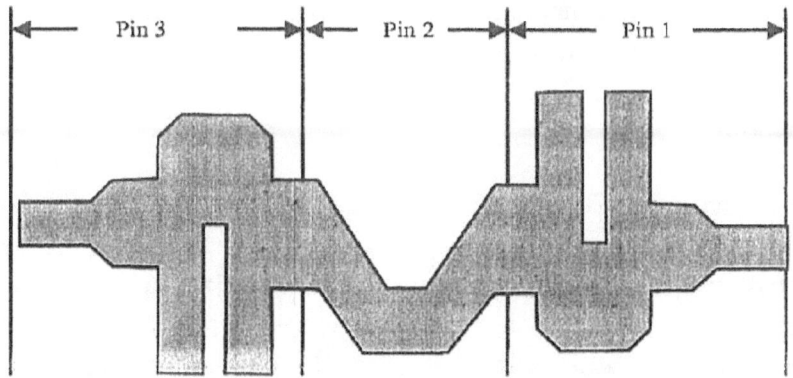

Fig 3.1 Crankshaft AX

Source: Dr Gondhalekar, 2019

Pins 2 and 3 were found to be free of porosity. The same pattern was evident in all the samples.

'Wow, the porosity appears exactly at the same spot!' Payal exclaimed with childlike enthusiasm. But Dr G was unmoved. He was like a demon possessed once the problem-solving got underway. Later, he explained to Payal that diagnosing the root cause with deductive logic required a still, meditative mind. It required a deep understanding of nature, he said, adding that the beautiful thing about nature was that it did not bend to the wishes of man. Nature's laws were absolute and immutable. Humans had to understand nature; humans had to figure out how the metal would flow and solidify.

Dr G asked for the table to be cleared. Fishing out a marker pen from his pocket, he divided the table into two halves. He requested the group to bring a sample of each product made in the foundry that had porosity as a frequently occurring defect and a sample of each product that did not have porosity as a defect. Samples were brought and placed on each side of the table. There, in front of them, was some curious evidence: that of crankshaft BY. It was a bit smaller than the one under study, which was called crankshaft AX. BY had only one flange and weighed less as it needed less metal. And it had no porosity. Payal quickly took a photograph of this evidence. Her mind was abuzz with the implications of this find, but Dr G was oblivious to the existence of anyone else at that moment.

Dr G then wanted to know which was the machine or die that produced the defective castings. The quality control manager began to hold forth, 'We have two furnaces. A furnace is specific to a particular grade of iron. Once the molten metal is at the desired temperature, it is poured into a ladle. The temperature is checked with a high-precision thermometer, and pouring is started. Pouring temperature has to be maintained between 1,400 and 1,440 degrees Celsius. One sure way of creating porosity is to pour at excessively low or excessively high temperatures. A temperature of 1,300 degrees, for instance, is sure to give porosity.

'The time between melting and pouring needs to be kept low. If molten metal is held too long, it oxidises in contact with oxygen from the air and becomes brittle. Pouring also has to be done at a fair clip. Observations have shown that pouring temperature drops from 1,430 to 1,350 degrees Celsius between the first and last moulds. I have been pressing for new better-insulated moulds, but the management is always strapped for funds.'

Dr G began to shuffle his feet, but the lady was on a roll now. It was not often that she met a man who commanded her respect, and she had to assist him. She had to tell him everything she knew.

'Pouring conditions are equally important. The rule for ideal pouring is pour quickly and uniformly with no interruptions. In answer to your query, young lady, cold shut occurs when pouring is interrupted. The metal poured earlier solidifies before the rest of the metal is poured in. At the 'junction', a discontinuity is created and presto! You have a cold shut.'

Dr G could not take it anymore. With a pained expression, he put the palms of his hands together and begged the lady to stop. He did not want to know anything more, he said. The astonished manager explained that she was only helping him by listing out the possible causes of porosity, but he was adamant.

'Information overload is as bad as or even worse than information scarcity,' he said to the group. Payal whistled softly and noted it down in a flash. 'It interrupts your logical thought processes and tempts you to stray away into specious arguments. It is the spam in your inbox, best deleted. When you have insufficient information, you will make the attempt to find what you need. If you have excess, however, you feel you know it all and you will not search. Then, no surprise, you will not find,' elaborated Dr G in his laconic style.

Dr G often remarked that, as an expert diagnostician, he brought to his client company the one thing that everybody in the company lacked: ignorance. He was quick to qualify that statement, however. It was ignorance born of wisdom, he said, as opposed to the ignorance of an illiterate fool. The problem in most companies was that too many people knew too much. They were unable to see what was right under their noses because they had too much dust in their eyes. 'I start with a clean slate every morning,' he declared. 'Pranayamas take all the stale air and previous impressions out of my system.'

The quality control manager was put off by the diagnostician's unwillingness to accept the information that she was presenting. Her image of the great diagnostician was developing a crack. But she decided to try out Dr G's way. 'Okay, I will provide only the information that you specifically ask for. What else you do you need?' she ended a bit timidly, sounding obviously hurt.

'How many dies do you have to make sand moulds of this product?' he asked, oblivious to the inflexions in her voice.

'Only one, and if you don't mind please, here we call it a pattern, not die. It is in two parts, male and female we call it,' interjected the pattern-making executive.

'How many ladles do you pour from each melt of the furnace?'

'Usually five ladles.'

'So each ladle is poured into sand moulds, and each of the sand moulds is made by the same pattern on the one and only one line that you have. Is that right?' Dr G asked.

'That is correct.'

'How do you make the mould?'

'Sand is poured into a box. The female half of the pattern makes an impression or cavity corresponding to one side of the product. Then the male half of the mould makes a cavity corresponding to the other side of the product. The two half-cavities are joined to give a complete cavity corresponding to the product. The metal is poured into the cavity. Does that suffice? We can go and see the patterns in the pattern maintenance section, if you wish.'

'Later, later. Now, only questions. After the mould has cooled, it is broken and the product is separated, right? Does it pass through only one line?'

'That is right. Only one line—I told you before. We have only one line!' Most people found Dr G's repetitive questions annoying in the extreme.

'Good! Now we are moving fast. Can you please find out if pouring from any particular ladle corresponds to more porosity defect and vice versa?'

'It will take some time. Shall we take a lunch break now?' Time had literally flown by, and they had not realised it.

'Okay, let us break for lunch, but please find out how the porosity on the AX shaft has varied with time. Look at your past records,' said Dr G.

Two hours later, they had the information. A widely held opinion was that the first ladle from each melt gave the lowest porosity in the casting because the furnace was the hottest and the sand was the coolest. Dr G refused to accept the opinion. At his insistence, data from the past few days was examined. It did not bear out the opinion. One team member went on to collect more historical data from the computerised archives. It showed that though porosity was widely prevalent, there was a period of about two months, during which fifty-four consecutive melts had shown no porosity. That was two years earlier, and one of the team members said that he distinctly remembered that it was the time when the new furnace was installed. He said that it was logical because the new furnace must have given good results, with good mixing of the additives and at the right temperature. Moreover, the new ladles that came with the furnace would have also ensured good pouring; both factors could contribute to porosity.

Payal noted another learning point in her diary: 'Get data firsthand. Look at the problem in detail before going into causes.' Dr G had put up the information on a board as it had come in. He now paused and stared at it for a long time without saying a word. The team members were busy with discussion amongst themselves, to which he was oblivious. Abruptly, emerging from his reveries, he called the group to order.

'Ladies and gentlemen, please look at the board and tell me, what do you see?' he said rather theatrically. 'Look at the data and tell me, what do you see?' he repeated.

Several comments were offered. Payal observed a curious phenomenon. Every time a cause was offered, Dr G would shake his head, refusing to accept it. He would repeat his favourite sentence, 'Look at the data. What do you see?' This went on for some time. Slowly, with an air of resignation, he turned to Payal and asked in a low voice, 'Can you see the most remarkable feature of the problem, Payal?'

Payal was pleased to be included into the discussion. 'I have remarked on it in my notebook as an interesting point, sir, but I am not sure what it implies. I have noted that the defect always occurs only in pin 1 and not in the other two pins. I also thought that the fact that it does not happen in pin 3 may be important because it looks similar to pin 1.'

'Very good. Also that it happens in AX but not BY.'

'But what does it imply, sir?'

'It means we have to look at what is different between pin 1 and pin 3 and what is different between AX and BY. Our root cause lies somewhere in the differences. Let us go and look at the pattern that makes the mould. We must examine the part of the pattern corresponding to pin 1 and pin 3 in detail and find out the differences. We must look at differences in the patterns of AX and BY too.'

The team trudged to the pattern maintenance shop and placed the male and female patterns side by side. They began to list out the differences:

1. Pin 1 was closer to the riser while pin 3 was farther away from it.
2. Pin 1 had metal entry from a thin shaft while pin 3 was at the last point of the metal flow into the thinnest shaft.
3. AX was bigger in size than BX. It would consume more metal.
4. The riser of AX was larger than that of BY.

5. The whole pattern of BY was at a lower lever from the pouring cup's position compared to AX.

As the teams were listing the differences, there was a commotion outside. One of the supervisors had come running with some startling information. He had detected porosity in crankshaft BY also! The team watched with bated breath, curious to see how Dr G would react.

For a moment, there was complete silence as Dr G absorbed the information. Then he calmly pronounced, 'Show me. Don't tell me. Show me!'

The supervisor walked out and reappeared with four samples of BY shafts—all with clearly visible porosity. Dr G looked carefully at them and then thumped the table in irritation. 'Why can't you, guys, give me correct data right in the beginning? Look, if you keep giving wrong data, nobody on earth can solve the problem. Henceforth, be careful. If you are not sure, say, "NOT SURE!" If you don't know, say, "DON'T KNOW"!' The entire group was startled by this sudden outburst.

'Anyway', he continued, calming down as rapidly as he had heated up, 'it makes one significant change in our approach from this point onwards. We now start looking at similarities between AX and BY. Ignore the differences! Let's get on with the job.' They continued examining similarities and differences and showing them to Dr G. After what seemed an interminable length of time, he straightened up and in a low resigned voice said there was only one really significant difference. 'Can you see it?' he asked all around.

The pattern-making expert was hardly listening. 'May I make a suggestion?' he asked. 'If we put a riser near the point of porosity, we can solve the problem because it will supply metal nearer to the point of demand during the shrinkage.'

To explain better, he brought a casting with its pouring cup, runner, and riser intact. It looked like figure 3.2.

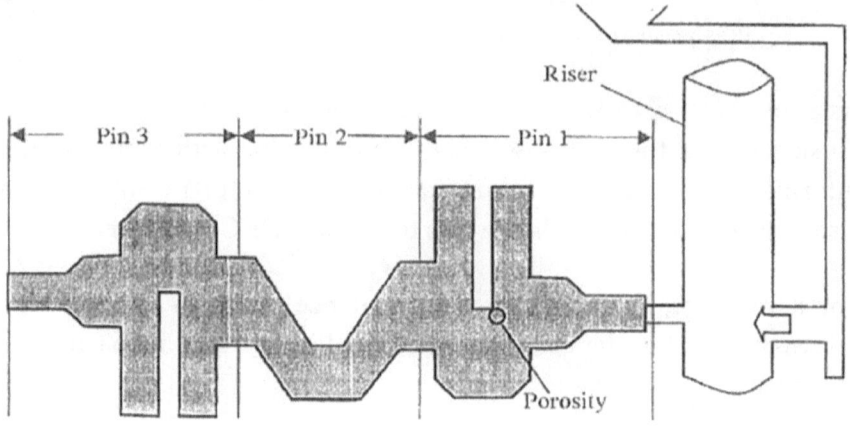

Fig 3.2

Source: Dr Gondhalekar, 2019

'Some time back', continued the pattern-making expert, 'we had faced the problem of porosity in both pin 1 and pin 3 in similar locations. I had raised the height of the riser and its volume, and the porosity in pin 3 had disappeared. I would have raised the volume of the riser even farther, but there is no space to accommodate it on the pattern. But now I have an idea. If we put another riser near the point of demand in pin 1, the porosity will disappear. I can do it by tonight.'

Dr G stopped him immediately, emphasising that no action would be allowed until completion of the diagnosis. He pointed out that the team needed to focus on one point, which was the only point of significance.

'The only significant difference between pin 1 and pin 3 lies in the distance from the riser. Pin 3 is farther while pin 1 is nearer to the riser. Their positions mean that the cooling would start from pin 3, and while it shrinks, it would draw metal from the pin 1 area, which in turn could draw from the riser. But as pin 1 solidifies, it would be unable to draw the metal it needs to make up for the inevitable shrinkage during solidification. Data shows that pin 1 is unable to draw metal from the riser.'

Dr G went on to elucidate, 'The whole question hinges on only one point: why does the riser succeed in supplying metal to pin 3 but somehow fails to supply to pin 1? The only difference between the two is that pin 3 demands the metal at an earlier point in time while pin 1 demands it at a later point in time. Now let us think over the question: what happens in that time interval?'

Slowly, as if waking up from a dream, the quality manager echoed the very words that were swirling in most people's minds. 'The riser, or its supply line, solidifies,' she whispered.

The diagnostic expert asked for a Vernier caliper, a measuring instrument. Placing it across the thinnest portion, he measured and found it to be 30mm in diameter. He marked the area with a chalk. Payal could not resist the temptation of clicking a close-up snapshot of that area with her digital camera. A sketch of it is shown in figure 3.3.

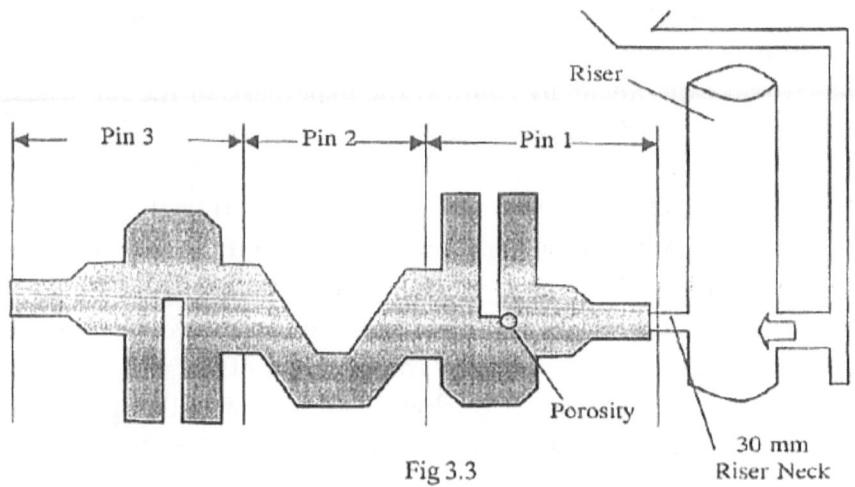

Fig 3.3

Source: Dr Gondhalekar, 2019

'Well, if thicker portions of the shaft can cool, why cannot the 30mm riser neck solidify?' inquired Dr G, adding that the root cause lay in the solidification of the riser neck happening prior to the solidification of pin 1.

One of the team members would not agree. He felt that the riser neck would be the last to solidify because it was joined to the huge mass of metal that constituted the riser. He argued that the concept of a riser was introduced in casting technology as a reservoir of metal that would remain molten till the very end and could therefore supply metal to the rest of the casting as it solidified and shrank. He said that the riser had been designed after numerous calculations and computer simulations, and it had been made even larger by the pattern-making expert to eliminate the porosity at pin 3. Early solidification of the riser or its neck was inconceivable. Moreover—and this was the clincher according to him—why did the riser neck not solidify in some cases? Why did they not get porosity on 100% of the shafts? Why was the riser neck partial to some shafts? He too was of the strongly considered opinion that an extra riser, suitably placed near the point of demand, would do the trick. He was a qualified metallurgist, and he knew what he was talking about.

Dr G refused to get drawn into the discussion. Noting that the day was now far advanced, he announced that they would reassemble on the shop floor the next day at 9 a.m. Tomorrow was D-Day, he told them. They would experimentally confirm the hypothesis of the root cause that he had proposed. Without further ado, he walked out of the factory.

The next morning, Dr G decided to conduct an experiment, where they would prevent solidification of the riser neck and confirm whether the porosity in pin 1 disappeared. Addressing the question of how to prevent early solidification of the riser neck, he found two alternatives emerging: one idea was to increase the diameter of the neck, and the other idea was to insulate it with a 'sleeve'. Unfortunately, though sleeves are known to the casting industry, standard sleeves of the required diameter were not readily available in the market. The pattern-making expert agreed to improvise a sleeve. It took him most of the day to make twenty improvised sleeves. Twenty were needed since it was decided to put one sleeve on each mould and experimentally verify for one full ladle. By 5 p.m. the sleeves were ready. Dr G then requested the team to stay back and personally observe insertion of the sleeves and entire experimental trial.

The team members distributed themselves around the pouring area. The moulds were made, the improvised sleeves were introduced, and the moulds were lined up on the casting machine, ready for the pouring. The quality manager explained to each team member what he or she had to observe. The molten metal was poured from the furnace into the ladle; the temperature was checked and found to be 1,425 degrees Celsius, which was within the specified range. Pouring was commenced. With all these preparations and so many management personnel observing and noting down his movements, the pouring operator became nervous. His pouring became non-uniform; the molten material spilt while pouring; the pouring time was high in one mould and low in another. It looked like every error in the book was occurring. When the temperature was measured after pouring the last mould, it had dropped as low as 1,270 degrees Celsius. The team was demoralised. This set of crankshafts was bound to be porous; casting technology dictated it. The quality manager courteously offered to repeat the pouring into another set of moulds.

But Dr G was unmoved. 'I don't care how the pouring was done as long as you observed how it was done. Just wait till the moulds cool, remove the castings from the sand, and check each and every one for porosity and other properties. Cut them at several places and make a thorough check. It does not matter if there is porosity. It is simply more learning,' he said and recommended they wind up for the day.

The team assembled again the next morning, except for the metallurgist, who walked in a minute late, triumphantly holding a crankshaft in his arms.

'Bad news for you, Dr G,' he beamed. 'I never believed your theory. At night, after everyone had left, I installed an extra riser near the point of demand in pin 1, with the help of my pattern-making colleagues. Well, friends, here is a crankshaft made with the extra riser, and it has no porosity! There really is no need for sleeves, as you can see!'

There was a stunned silence as every eye turned to Dr G. Surely, this was going to be the most embarrassing moment in his life. To their surprise, he calmly thanked the metallurgist, asking him to place his sample aside, and asked everyone to avoid getting distracted. 'Please continue focusing on yesterday's experimental crankshafts. Please cut them and check thoroughly for porosity.'

Meekly, the team trickled out and got down to the job of cutting and testing the samples of the previous day. Beckoning Payal to accompany him, Dr G moved with the team to the cutting machine. The pallet load of twenty castings was ready. The first casting was being loaded. 'Stop!' cried Dr G. 'Which one are you cutting?' It was number 1.

'No, no, take it down. Cut number 20 first. It had the lowest pouring temperature, below 1,300 degrees Celsius, and its pouring conditions were pretty bad. It should be the worst of the lot. Cut that first. If it turns out to be free of porosity, then we can be reasonably sure that the rest are also good. We will get an idea of the results most rapidly that way.'

The twentieth shaft was duly loaded onto the cutting machine. All the team members crowded around. Payal was anxious. The reputation of her professor depended upon what the cutting machine would reveal in the next few minutes. As the shaft parted in two, the quality manager grabbed it. She whooped with joy like a little girl and almost flung the piece into the air. 'No porosity!' she screamed.

In a voice completely devoid of emotion, Dr G said, 'Cut number 19, and go backwards till every one of them is cut.' Then he walked away to the pattern-making room and began to examine the pattern in detail. Payal followed him.

'Sir, aren't you curious about the result of the others?'

'Not at all. The results are bound to be the same. After all, I have applied stringent deductive logic to analyse the root cause. How can it be wrong?'

There he goes! thought Payal to herself. *Blowing his own trumpet again.*

Before he could say anything further, there was another commotion. A team member came rushing in, holding a cut piece, shouting excitedly, 'It has porosity! It has porosity!'

In a heart-stopping moment, Dr G had snatched the sample from his hand and was looking minutely at the porous portion. 'It cannot be,' he said with supreme confidence. 'This crankshaft could not have been made with the insulating sleeve.'

'No, no, I am referring to the crankshaft made with the extra riser!' panted the team member. 'Not the one with sleeve. I brought it from the batch that had the extra riser.'

The disgruntled metallurgist, who had installed the extra riser and who had triumphantly displayed the one good piece he had got, was cutting more pieces made from the extra riser. It was one of those that had been cut and found to be porous. Dr G's theory remained proven.

As reports of each sample being cut came in, it became clearer and clearer that the sleeve had indeed worked. Not a single one of the twenty had the slightest porosity; analysis of microstructure, hardness, and other properties revealed that those twenty were the finest-quality crankshafts ever produced from his foundry.

The metallurgist was found to have gone home due to an urgent summon from his wife. It turned out that only three out of the fifty shafts that he had cast with the extra riser had no porosity. By a lucky chance, the first one he had cut was one of the three.

Finally, everything fell in place. Dr G explained to them how they were able to draw a sample of five good pieces in the old inspection system. After the castings had cooled, when the sand moulds were broken, they passed through a sand-separating system, where the castings got jumbled up. When they came out of the system, there was no way of knowing which one was poured first. If the first few castings poured were withdrawn as samples, they perhaps tended to be free of porosity; as the temperature of the pouring dropped, the porosity increased. It was all a matter of sampling, he said, adding that this was referred to as type II error in statistical research methodology.

It was on the evening of the third day, as Dr G and Payal were returning, that she inquired, 'I admired the way you were so cool about the riser report. How were you so confident?'

'It was easy. I had a close look at the neck of the additional riser. It was small. It was bound to solidify. I was sure that the good piece was only a chance occurrence. Most people are unable to distinguish between chance causes and assignable causes. I was sure that subsequent samples would fail. And even if they did not, it would simply be a source of more data for us to understand the behaviour of the metal.'

'But whatever you may say, sir, on the whole it was a brilliant performance!' Payal's face was radiant.

'Yes, it was a rather tough case. But if you hang around, Payal, this will turn out to be nothing.'

With this remark, Dr G slouched in the car and began to stare out of the window at the passing scenery. He was already thinking of the next case.

Appendix 5

Inspiring Learning to Develop Talent Requirement for Smart Manufacturing Implementation

Major Dr J. Prebagaran, Ph.D. (Founder and CEO, SMC Professional Center for Learning & Development)

Introduction

The potential for smart manufacturing to significantly improve manufacturing capability and capacity is real. However, it will remain as potential if organisations do not develop required talents to implement smart manufacturing. According to the National Institute of Standards and Technology (NIST), smart manufacturing is a system that is 'fully-integrated, collaborative manufacturing systems that respond in real time to meet changing demands and conditions in the factory, in the supply network, and in customer needs'. The amazing systems of smart manufacturing are great enablers to revolutionise manufacturing.

Experienced learning facilitators will be aware that learners will have a different level of motivation. Some learning psychologists categorise motive for learning into surface, deep, and achieving. When the motivation to learn is only surface level, learners attend the class merely to meet the minimal criteria for attendance requirement.

One of the key responsibilities of learning facilitators is to inspire learners to appreciate the benefits of learning to be a high-VA member of their organisation. In the smart manufacturing context, the learner must be aware of the requirements to use real-time data and technology when, where, and in the forms that are needed by people and machine. While access to data is available to almost anybody, we need competent workforce to analyse and create meaning from the data. Merely thirty years ago, having access to data meant power. But today, having power means knowing what to ignore and what to *focus*. Smart manufacturing could not afford employees who are drowning with data but starving for wisdom.

This chapter will provide practical approach to inspire learning to develop talent requirement for smart manufacturing.

Inspiring Learning with Effective Instructional System Design

You wouldn't walk into your doctor's clinic for her to say hello and write prescription before diagnosis. Ability to diagnose the complex human system and decide appropriate prescription based on the data analysis is what makes the medical profession challenging and noble. Just like the medical profession, learners should expect a training programme based on sound instructional system design.

In the context of smart manufacturing, the instructional system design may start with task analysis. A task analysis is a systemic collection of data about a specific job or group of jobs to determine what an employee should be taught and the resources required to achieve optimal performance. The framework in figure 1 propose business needs as the first step to determine the training needs. The model emphasised the requirement to ensure vertical integration of organisation's business needs, job performance needs, training needs, and required competency to perform the job. By adopting this model, an organisation could ensure customisation and alignment of training for performance improvement.

The model incorporated performance analysis needs and the four levels of evaluation proposed by Kirkpatrick (2007). Right questions will be a valuable guide to develop effective training.

Figure 1. Integrated Instructional System Design

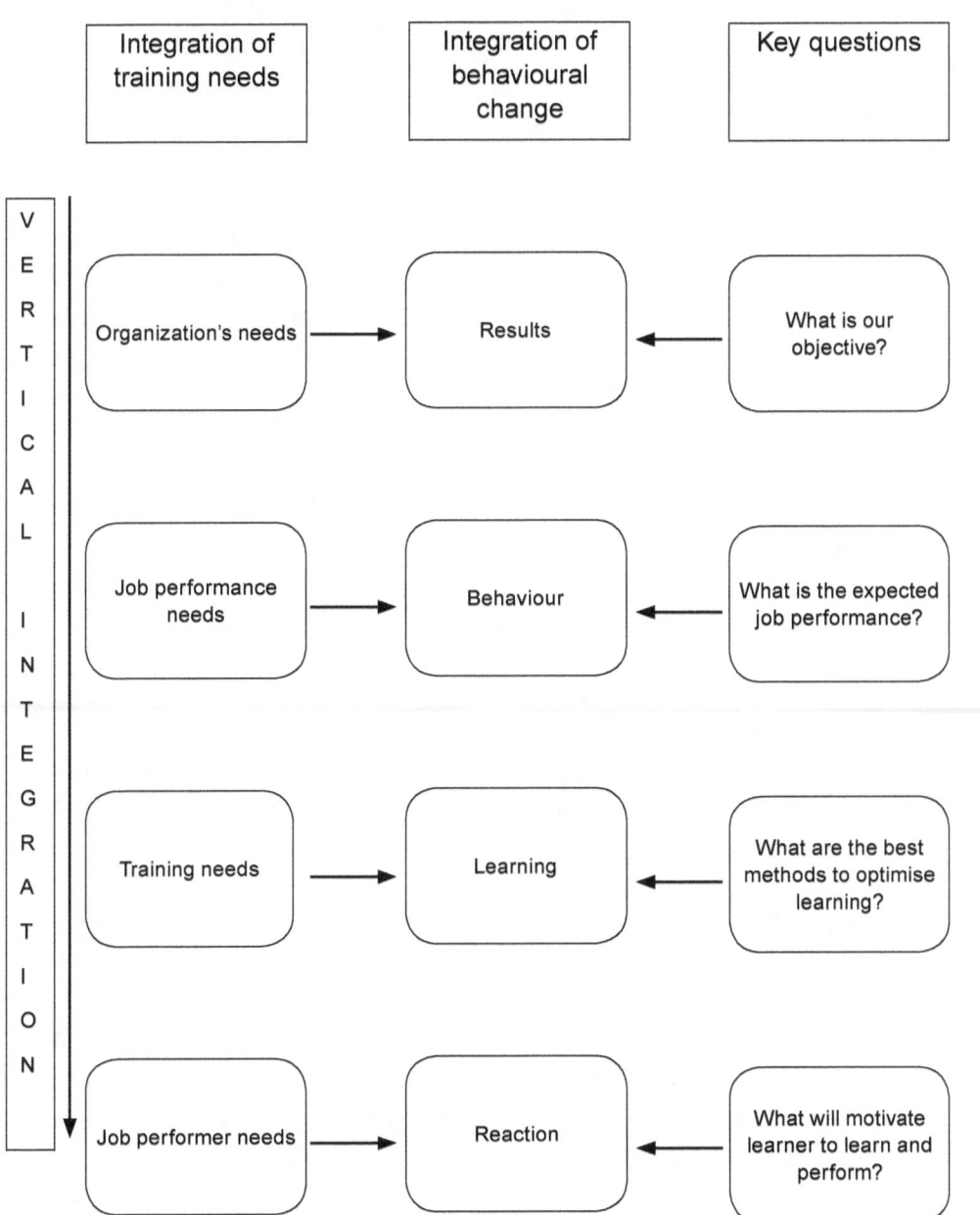

Source: Dr J. Prebagaran

Legendary management consultant Peter Drucker reflects on the power of question: 'My greatest strength as a consultant is to be ignorant and ask a few questions.' The model emphasised the requirement to meet individual needs by asking, 'What will motivate them to learn and perform?' This question is valuable to ensure instructional system design focuses on inspiring learners and not merely giving instruction.

Remember, smart manufacturing is not your goal. The goal of an organisation is to *win* in the hypercompetitive business world to satisfy the requirements of demanding stakeholders. Smart manufacturing is the method adopted to achieve your business goals. The ability to meet the demand for competitive cost, highest quality, and excellent services will determine survival for any organisation.

An effective instructional system designer will should and answer the following key questions:

- **What are our organisation's business objectives?**

    This question will seek the answer for expected business results. Obviously, the answer to this question will require input from various functional experts. Smart organisation will understand that talent development is an interdependent activity managed by L&D department.

- **What is the expected job performance to achieve the business objectives?**

    This question will enable the instructional system designer to determine the expected job performance and behaviour. The data for the job performance indicator will be amongst the key inputs for this process.

- **What are the best methods to optimise?**

    This question will enable the instructional system designer to incorporate suitable activities that optimise learners' experience.

The learners' career background, aptitude, and academic background will be valuable input for this process.

- **What will motivate learner to learn and perform?**

This question will enable the instructional system designer to determine relevant learning activities, content, and levels of learning that motivate learners. The ability to understand the 'motive for action' of the learners could be a great source of motivation for learning.

What are the unique skills required for smart manufacturing?

The manufacturing industry has always evolved to be smarter and smarter. Thus, the workforce has acquired various skills or 'tribal knowledge' to satisfy demanding requirements to manage cost competition while ensuring highest customer satisfaction and value for money. However, smart manufacturing requires certain unique talents. The unique talent requirement for smart manufacturing will certainly differ from organisation to organisation. The first step for any organisation to develop talent is to systematically determine the unique skill to meet the skill demand for smart manufacturing. Amongst the commonly cited unique skills for smart manufacturing are the following:

- **Analytical thinking**—smart manufacturing requires disciplined analysis of data to determine optimum manufacturing operational strategies. Employees must be competent to use real-time data and technology to make well-aligned decisions with organisation's strategies. These strategies are vital to survive the hypercompetitive manufacturing environment.
- **Integrated knowledge**—the advanced manufacturing system for smart manufacturing cannot survive the siloed mentality. The use of real-time data and technology when, where, and in the form needed by people and machines requires the workforce to understand the value of data from other departments. Imagine an engineering team responsible for the installation of a new production system. The knowledge

and appreciation of production schedule will be vital to develop the planned maintenance schedule for the equipment. Knowledge of the current technical skill of the technician will be valuable to determine additional training requirement to optimise the new machine to ensure a smooth operation. As such, the engineering team training will include production schedule and new skill requirement besides the technical knowledge of the new production system. This knowledge about production schedule and current skill will certainly improve the opportunity for better collaboration amongst interrelated departments, which is vital for survival in smart manufacturing.

- **Digital diagnostics and analytics**—the routine job of manufacturing like stacking, picking, packing, or racking can be easily done by programmable robots with higher degree of efficiency than us humans. Human capability is very much more valuable than these routine tasks. The workforce of smart manufacturing will require skill to configure, maintain, operate, and repair smart machines by utilising smart tools and technology.
- **Decision making**—smart manufacturing demands shifting from managing based on opinion to managing based on facts. The availability of data-capturing devices and machines on the plant floor with information system will require the workforce with the ability to act on quantifiable data rather than instinct. Making sense of huge amount of data will require big-data analytical skill. Without big-data analytical skill, employees will be drowning with data but starving for wisdom required to make the right decision.
- **Digitally capable workforce**—smart manufacturing equips the workforce with a highly sophisticated toolkit to operate sophisticated equipment or system. Employees require relevant skillsets to optimise these tools including compliance on the recommended operation and maintenance guidelines.

Achieve Manufacturing Excellence Lean and Smart Manufacturing | 127

Acquiring the unique skill required for an organisation is a dynamic process. Technology and work processes will be continuously improved. Thus, the unique skillset required shall be continuously updated.

Why a Competency Dictionary Is essential for Talent Development

Once the list of unique talents is finalised, a competency dictionary describing these competencies for different levels of employees should be developed. A competency dictionary is a document that lists competencies needed to cover the job within an organisation. Since work processes could be unique to respective organisations, each organisation should have its own competency dictionary. Generally, the competency dictionary will consist of the following information:

- Competency title
- Competency definition (this defines in more detail what the competency is about)
- Competency level (this shows the increasing sophistication or complexity at which the competency can be demonstrated)
- Behavioural indicators (these provide details on specific behaviours for the competencies at each level, providing examples of how competency can be demonstrated)
  Warning signs and positive indicators (these are positive and negative behaviours to be)

Competency is the ability of an employee to perform certain tasks with required level of proficiency defined by the organisation. Palan (2003) described the significance of determining required competency to ensure effective talent management. Competency will focus on factors the organisation has identified as vital to achieve its objectives. Competencies are generally divided into three categories as shown in table 1.

Table 1: Categories of Competencies

S/No	Competency	Description	Example
1.	Core competency	It's an organisation's unique strength often stated in their values. Every employee is expected to demonstrate their core competencies.	Simplicity is a core value of Apple as 'it takes a lot of hard work to make something simple, to truly understand the underlying challenges and come up with elegant solution'.
2.	Functional competency	These are skills that employees require to perform their specific function according to the required standards and conditions. Data analysis is an example of functional competency of a technician for smart manufacturing.	It is able to compare, contrast, and combine information to determine association between seemingly independent events to recognise trends and possible cause-effect relationship.
3.	Behavioural competency	It is any behaviour such as teamwork or leadership skills required for effective executing of their job. Behavioural competency is vital for smooth transition of work process. In the context of smart manufacturing, teamwork is a critical behavioural competency to ensure integrated work processes in an interdependent work environment.	Employees collaborate within and across departments to achieve the desired results.

Source: Dr J. Prebagaran

An example of competency dictionary is shown in table 2.

Table 2: Competency Dictionary

Competency Title: Analytical Thinking

Competency definition	Why it is important
Analytical thinking is about bringing disciplined analysis to data and situations to see cause and effect and make effective decision for smart manufacturing.	This is important in enabling us to prioritise and take important decisions based on an assessment of the impact and implication of the likely outcomes to achieve smart manufacturing objectives.

Source: Dr J. Prebagaran

Level 1 (foundational)	Level 2 (basic)	Level 3 (intermediate)	Level 4 (advanced)	Level 5 (expert)
Awareness and ability to apply the competency in routine work situation	Basic understanding and ability to apply competency in routine and varied work situations of limited difficulty	Solid understanding and ability to apply the competency in a full range of work situation	Deep understanding and ability to apply the competency in a full range of work situation	Complete understanding and ability to apply the competency creatively in the most complex situation
Breaks problems into simple lists of tasks, activities, or issues to be addressed in the context of smart manufacturing environment	Recognises and reviews the relevant factors of a situation or problem to determine basic pattern for routine manufacturing decisions	Analyses pros and cons and establishes basic priorities and relationships for full range of work process in smart manufacturing environment	Uses analytical techniques to break a complex problem into component parts for complex manufacturing decisions	Breaks multidimensional abstract problems into component parts to determine the role that different parts of the system play so new solutions can be derived in complex manufacturing environment

A competency dictionary will provide the organisation specific guidelines to determine observable and measurable behaviours expected from the employees. An organisation can determine the competency description for each level based on its respective business process. This will certainly guide in the process of instructional system design or informal learning by self-directed learners. As such, a competency dictionary can assist in inspiring learners.

How to Determine Competency Gap

Competency gap is defined as the difference between current competency level and the required competency level of a job holder. It is common for managers to have different expectations based on their respective personal standards. Thus, a clearly defined and common interpretation of the definition is valuable.

The first step to determine competency gap is to define the required competency level for each position. For example, an organisation may determine that an entry-level process engineer requires analytical thinking competency at level 2. A job holder's competency will be assessed based on their ability to demonstrate the required competency with reference to the competency dictionary. It is vital to provide required training for the assessor to enable reliable and valid assessment of current competency level of job holder.

Job holders' view and feedback is vital for their 'buy-in' of the outcome of competency gap assessment. Adults will be inspired to learn if they are ready and driven by their own motivation.

How to Determine Training Intervention that Inspires Learners

The output from the competency gap assessment will be input to determine training intervention. Experienced facilitators will be aware that performance improvement will require both training and non-training intervention.

Training intervention is a strategy when the factors affecting performance is due to a competency gap. In other words, the job holder does not have the required skill, knowledge, and attitude to perform the task at the required standard.

Experience will tell you that a performance problem may not necessarily be due to competency issue. Sometimes a performance issue is not because we don't know what to do but because don't do what we know! For example, data-driven decision making is expected in smart manufacturing. While your data analyst may be an expert in optimising data-crunching applications, decisions are often subject to human biases. We may trust and rely on data that support our expectation or position. Managing biasness may be related to value systems that require non-training intervention. Combination of training and non-training intervention is critical to inspire your talent to improve performance.

Application of Bloom's Taxonomy to Develop Desired Learning Outcome

One of the key considerations in designing an effective training programme is determining the learning outcome. Learning outcomes are statements of what a learner is expected to demonstrate after completion of a learning process. Description in competency dictionary will be valuable to write your learning outcome. One of the fundamental guidelines to write learning outcome is based on Bloom's taxonomy. Bloom's taxonomy is a hierarchical ordering of cognitive processes. The main purpose of Bloom's taxonomy is to classify learning outcome from lower-order thinking skills to higher-order thinking skills.

Bloom's taxonomy will be valuable in inspiring learners by developing the desired learning outcome. For example, the current competency of a learner could be at the level called "Understand". The learner is able to explain basic pattern for routine manufacturing decision, which is in level 2 of competency dictionary. If the required competency of the learner is level 3, the learning outcome can be written as an execution of the full range of smart manufacturing process for quality assurance. A well-written learning outcome is critical to develop learning activities and assessment of learners. Thus, fundamental knowledge of Bloom's taxonomy is a vital for an instructional system designer. Effective design is critical to implement a good training that inspires learners.

Inspire Learners with Application of Adult Learning Principles

Malcolm Knowles's adult learning principles or andragogy had been adopted by learning and development professionals to inspire learning (Elwood F. Holton, 2015). Learning and development professionals should be aware of the implication of adult learning principles in inspiring learning. Practical application of adult learning principles is imperative to ensure effective learning happens. Experienced facilitators will be aware that no learning will happen without the learner's 'buy-in'. Malcolm Knowles is amongst the leading educationists and is well known for his contributions in promoting adult learning methodology for effective learning. Table 3 shows Malcolm Knowles's five assumptions of adult learners.

Table 3: Malcolm Knowles's Five Assumptions of Adult Learners

S/No	Characteristics of adult learners	Description
1.	**Self-Concept**	As a person matures, his/her self-concept moves from one of being a dependent personality towards one of being a self-directed human being.
2.	**Adult learner experience**	As a person matures, he/she accumulates a growing reservoir of experience that becomes an increasing resource for learning.
3.	**Readiness to learn**	As a person matures, his/her readiness to learn becomes oriented increasingly to the developmental tasks of his/her social roles.

4	Orientation to learning	As a person, matures his/her time perspective changes from one of postponed application of knowledge to immediacy of application. As a result, his/her orientation towards learning shifts from one of subject centredness to one of problem centredness.
5.	Motivation to learn	As a person matures, the motivation to learn is internal.

Source: Dr J. Prebagaran

The facilitator will be able to inspire learners by incorporating these characteristics of adult learning. Examples are e-learning platforms that provide flexible learning to enable the learners to decide what I want to study, where I want to study, when I want to study, and what I want to study. These characteristics will satisfy the self-concept described by Knowles.

Adults experience will be a valuable to inspire learning. Facilitators shall be familiar with relevant experience of learners and optimise these experiences to enhance learning. Learning activities like case studies will be effective tools to enable adults to optimise their experience.

Adults will be inspired to learn concepts that are practical now. As such, the desired learning outcomes and learning activities that focus on immediate application will inspire adult learners.

The ability to describe the benefits of the learning to address the problems of smart manufacturing will inspire adults; facilitators may create case studies of challenges of smart manufacturing due to competency issues. Adults will be inspired when they know the benefits of learning to manage these problems.

Facilitators should be aware of both internal and external sources of motivation of adults. The ability to analyse valuable information for effective decision making could be a source of motivation for adults. The value of the learning to prepare them for a higher position will also be a great source motivation. Learning facilitators should be aware of the motivation source of learners.

Why Effective Feedback Is Critical to Inspire Learners

Assessment is an integral part of training. Assessment is a great opportunity for providing feedback. Giving feedback can be challenging, especially when the learners are not meeting the expected learning outcome. A good feedback could be a source of inspiration.

Carol Dweck (2008) shared the story of a Chicago school where students were given the grade 'Not Yet' if they are yet to meet the passing requirement for the assessment. Instead of branding the student as failed, 'not yet' provides hope. Feedback with following criteria could inspire learning:

- Feedback should be focused and has clear direction for action. General statements like *adequate*, *good*, and *excellent* should be avoided.
- Feedback should be timely. Rather than at the end of the learning programme, feedback must be given along the journey of learning process. This will enable learners to take corrective action for improvement.
- Feedback should create a positive experience. Facilitators should look for opportunity for what is right besides suggestion on area for improvement.

Given well, feedback will be a great source for inspired learning to develop talent in the hypercompetitive smart manufacturing world.

How to Improve Learning Transfer from Classroom to Workplace

Learning transfer can be defined as the ability of a learner to successfully apply the behaviour, knowledge, and skill acquired in a learning event to the job, with a resulting improvement in job performance. Experiencing improvement could be a great source of inspiration for learners. An organisation with a desire to maximise the value from training will be aware that creating a conducive environment to apply the lesson learnt is essential. Training should be treated as a performance improvement project with clearly defined post-training activities. The 70:20:10 model helps integrate formal classroom training with coaching and workplace application. The model was developed in the 1980s by researchers at the Center for Creative Leadership, USA (Bob Elchinger and Mike Lombardo,1996).

Here are some types of information according to the model:

- **70% of learning is experiential.** It happens through daily tasks, challenges, and practice.
- **20% of learning is social.** It happens with and through other people, like coaching and mentoring with experienced co-workers.
- **10% of learning is formal.** It happens through structured training courses and programmes.

Well-integrated formal classroom learning, coaching, and mentoring programme and application of learning will be a great source of inspiration to learners.

Public Recognition as a Source of Inspiration

Workplace training can be conducted in collaboration with universities leading to professional qualifications. Many universities worldwide have dedicated units for executive development. A good partnership between industry experts and university academicians will create synergy to develop industry-relevant programmes to meet academic rigorousness. Public recognition in the form of graduation ceremony is one of the sources of inspiration especially for working adults who missed tertiary learning opportunities.

Conclusion

The benefits of workplace training need no introduction. In the context of smart manufacturing, which demands various new skillsets, workplace training maybe mandatory for survival. However, some employees may not be inspired to learn for a variety of reasons; they may fear stepping out of their comfort zone in the process of learning new skills. The learner's past experience in training environment may not have been inspiring. In some organisations, employees are instructed to attend mandated training. Do you think instruction inspires learning? Obviously, no. No matter the perception of learners, learning facilitators are responsible to inspire learning.

Here's a quote by William Arthur Ward:

The mediocre teachers tells.

The good teacher explains.

The superior teacher demonstrates.

The great teacher inspires.

References

Abair, R. A. (1997). Agile manufacturing: successful implementation strategies. Annual International Conference Proceedings ± American Production and Inventory Control Society, 218-219.

Ahlstrom, A. P., and Westbrook, R. (1999). Implications of mass customization for operations management: An exploratory survey. International Journal of Operations & Production Management, 19(3), 262-274.

Ahmad S., Schroeder, R,G., Mallick, D, N. (2010). The relationship among modularity, functional coordination, and mass customization, European Journal of Innovation Management, 13 (1), 46-61.

Anderson, D. M. (1997). Agile product development for mass customization. New York: McGraw-Hill.

Anderson, D. M. (2004). Build to order and mass customization. Cambria, California: CIM Press.

Argyris, C. (1964). Integrating the Individual and the Organization. New York: John Wiley and Sons.

Atzeni, E., Luliano, L., Minetola, P., Salmi, A. (2010). Redesign and cost estimation of rapid manufacturing plastic parts. Rapid Prototyping Journal, 16 (5), 308-317.

Bessant, J., Francis, D., Meredith, S., Kaplinsky, R. and Brown, S. (2001). 'Developing manufacturing agility in SMEs', International Journal of Technology Management, 22 (1/2/3), 28-54.

Blanche, T. M., and Durrheim, K. (1999). Research in practice: Applied methods for the social sciences. Cape Town: UCT Press.

Boer, C.R., Pedrazzoli, P., Bettoni, A., Sorlini, M. (2013). Mass Customization and Sustainability. Springer, NY.

Brandyberry, A., Rai, A. and White, G.P. (1999). "Intermediate performance impacts of advanced manufacturing technology systems: an empirical investigation", Decision Sciences, 30 (4), 933-1020.

Brown, S. and Bessant, J. (2003). 'The manufacturing strategy – capabilities links in mass customization and agile manufacturing – an exploratory study', International Journal of Operations and Productions Management, 23 (7), 707-30.

Stump, B., Badurdeen, F. (2012). Integrating Lean and Other Strategies for Mass Customization Manufacturing: a case study. Journal of Intelligent Manufacturing, 23, 109-124.

Cameron, K., & Freeman, S. (1989). Cultural congruence, strength and type; Relationship to effectiveness. Academy of Management Annual Convention, August 1989, Washington DC.

Cavana, R. Y., Delahaye, B. L., and Sekaran, U. (2001). Applied business research: qualitative and quantitative methods. Australia: Wiley & Sons

Chandler, A. (1962). Strategy and Structure: Chapters in the History of the American Industrial Enterprise, Irwin, Boston, MA.

Chandler, A. (1992). 'Corporate strategy, structure and control methods in the United States during the 20th century', Industrial and Corporate Change, 1 (2), 263-84.

Christopher, M. and Towill, D.R. (2000). 'Supply chain migration from lean and functional to agile and customized', Supply Chain Management, 5 (4), 206-13.

Cigolini, R., Pero, M., Rossi, T., Sianesi, A. (2014). Linking supply chain configuration to supply chain performance; a discreet event simulation model. Simul Modell Practice Theory, 40, 1-11.

Coates, T. D. (1998). The paperless laboratory: an integrated environment for data acquisition, analysis, archiving and collaboration, trends in research. New York, NY: Plenum Press.

Crocitto, M.,Youssef,M. (2003). The Human Side of Organizational Agility, Industrial Management & Data Systems, 103 (6), 388-397

Da Silveira, G., Borenstein, D., & Fogliatto, F.S. (2001). Mass Customization: Literature review and research directions. International Journal of Production Economics, 77, 1-3.

Deal, T. and Kennedy, A. (1982). Corporate Cultures: The Rites and Rituals of Corporate Life, Addison-Wesley, Reading, MA.

Denison, D. R. (1990). Corporate culture and organizational effectiveness New York: Wiley.

Denison, D. R., Janovics, J., Young, J., & Cho, H. J. (2006). Diagnosing organizational cultures: validating a model and method. Working paper, International Institute for Management Development, Lausanne, Switzerland.

Denzin, N. K. (1989). Interpretive interactionism. Applied Social Research Method Series. Newbury Park, CA: Sage.

Devor, R., Mills, J.J. (1997). Agile Manufacturing Research: accomplishments and opportunities. IEE Transactions, 29 (10), 813-824.

Dove, R. (1995). Presentation made at the Benchmarking for Agility Workshop, Automation and Robotics Research Institute, Fort Worth, TX.

Dowlatshahi, s., Cao, Q. (2005). The impact of alignment between enterprise and information technology on business performance in an agile manufacturing environment. Journal of Operations Management, 20, 531-550.

Duguay, C., Landry, S. and Pasin, F. (1997). From mass production to flexible/agile production, International Journal of Operations & Production Management, 17 (12), 1183-95.

Duray, R. (2002). Mass Customisation origins: Mass or custom manufacturing. International Journal of Operations & Production Management, 22 (3), 314-328.

Easterby-Smith, M., and Thorpe, R., and Lowe, A. (1991). Management Research. London: Sage.

Elsass, P. and Veiga, J. (1994), 'Acculturation in acquired organizations: a force field perspective', Human Relations, 47 (4), 431-53.

Feitzinger, E., and Lee, H. L. (1997). Mass customization at Hewlett-Packard: the power of postponement. Harvard Business Review, 75 (1), 116-121.

Felin, T., Foss, N, J., Heimeriks, K, H., Madsen, T, L. (2012). Microfoundations of routines and capabilities; individuals, process and structure. Journal of Management Studies, 49 (8), 1351-1374.

Ferguson,S,M., Olewnik,A,T.,Cormier,P (2014) A Review of Mass Customization Across Marketing, Engineering And Distribution Domains Toward Development of A Process Framework, Research in Engineering Design, 25 (1), 11-30.

Fogliato, F,S; Silviera, G,J,C, 2011, Mass Customization; Engineering and Managing Global Operations, Spinger, London.

Forrester, R. (1995), Implications of lean manufacturing for human resource strategy, Work Study, 44 (3), 20-24.

Gandhi, A;Magar,C;Roberts,R (2014). How Technology Can Drive The Nest Wave of MassCustomization, www.mckinsey.com/.../ MOBT32_02-09_MassCustomization accessed on 23rd Dec 2014

Gilmore, J. H., and Pine, B. J. (1997). The four faces of mass customization. Harvard Business Review, 75 (1), 91-101.

Goldhar, J. D., and Jelinek, M. (1983). Plan for economies of scope. Harvard Business Review, 61 (6), 141-148.

Gondhalekar, S., and Karamchandani, V. (1994). Robust Kaizen Systems. The TQM Magazine, 6 (3), 5-8.

Gosling, J., Purvisa, L., Naima, M, M. (2010). Supply chain flexibility as a determinant of supplier selection. International Journal of Production Economics, 128 (1), 11-21.

Gould, P. (1997). What is agility. Manufacturing Engineer, 76 (1), 28-31.

Gunasekaran, A and Yusuf, Y,Y. (2002). Agile Manufacturing; A Taxonomy of Strategic and Technological Imperatives, International Journal of Production Research, 40 (6), 1357-1385

Hallgreen, M., Olhager J. (2009). Lean and Agile Manufacturing: External and Internal Drivers and Performance Outcomes, International Journal of Production and Operations Management, 29 (10), 976-999

Hamel, G., and Prahalad, C. (1994). Competing for future. Boston, MA: Harvard Business Press.

Hart, C. W. (1995). Mass Customization: Conceptual underpinning, opportunities and limits. International Journal of Service Industry Management, 6 (2), 36-45.

Hart, C. W. (1996). Made to Order. Marketing Management, 5 (2), 12-22.

Hayes, R., and Wheelwright, S. (1984). Restoring our competitive edge. New York, NY: Wiley & Sons.

Hines, P., Holweg, M., and Rich, N. (2004). Learning to evolve: A review of contemporary Lean thinking. International Journal of Operations and Production Management, 24 (10), 994 – 1011.

Hofstede, G. (1995). 'Cultural constraints in management theories', in Wren, J. (Ed.), The Leadership Companion: Insights on Leadership through the Ages, Free Press, New York, NY.

Huang, X., Kristal, M.M. and Schroeder, R.G. (2008). 'Linking learning and effective process implementation to mass customization capability', Journal of Operations Management, 26 (5), 714-29.

Huang, X., Kristal, M.M. and Schroeder, R.G. (2010). The impact of organizational structure on mass customization capability; a contingent perspective. Production and Operations Management, 19 (5), 515-530.

Huffman, C., and Kahn, B. (1998). Variety for sale: Mass customization or mass confusion. Journal of retailing, 74, 491-513.

Imai, Masaaki (1991). Kaizen – The key to Japan's competitive success. Singapore: McGraw-Hill.

Ireland, R.D. and Hitt, M.A. (1999). Achieving and maintaining strategic competitiveness in the 21st century: the role of strategic leadership, The Academy of Management Executive, 13 (1), 43-57.

Liker, J.K. (2004). The Toyota Way 14 Management Principles. New York: McGraw-Hill.

Kahn, K. B. (1998). Benchmarking sales forecasting performance measures. Journal of Business Forecasting, Winter (1998-1999), 19-23.

Kanter, R.M. (1992). The Change Masters, Routledge, London.

Katayama, H., Bennett, D. (1996). Lean Production in a changing competitive world: A Japanese perspective. International Journal of Operations and Production Management, 16 (2), 8-23.

Kekre, S., Srinivasan, K. (1990). Broader Product line: A necessity to achieve success. Management Science, 36, 1216-1231.

Kidd, P. T. (1996). Agile manufacturing: a strategy for the 21st century. IEE Colloquium (Digest), 74, 6.

Lai, F., Zhang, M., Lee, D., Zhao, X. (2012). The impact of supply chain integration on mass customization capability; an extended resource-based view IEET Trans, Engineering Management, 59 (3), 443-456.

Lamming, R. (1993). Beyond Partnership, Prentice-Hall, Hemel Hempstead.

Lampel, J., and Mintzberg, H. (1996). Customizing customization. Sloan Management Review, 38, 21-30.

Lawler, E. E. (1986). High involvement management: Participative strategies for improving organizational performance. San Francisco, CA: Jossey-Bass Inc.

Lazonick, W. (1991). Business Organization and the Myth of the Market Economy, Harvard University Press, Cambridge MA.

Leffakis,Z,M,.Dwyer,D,J (2014). The effects of human resource systems on operational performance in mass customization manufacturing environments, Production Planning and Control: The management of Operations, 25 (15).

Liao,K., Ma, Z., Lee J, Y., Ke, K. (2011). Achieving Mass Customization Through Trust Driven Information Sharing: A Suppliers Perspective, Management Research Review, 34 (5), 541-552.

Liu, G., Shah, R., Schroeder, R, G. (2011). The relationship among functional integration, mass customization and firm performance. International Journal of Production Research, 50 (3), 677-690.

Lindorff, M. (2001). Are they lonely at the top? Social relationship and social support among Australian managers. Work and Stress, 15 (3), 274-282.

Liu, G., Shah R., Schroeder, R, S. (2010). Managing Demand and Supply Uncertainties to achieve Mass Customization ability, Journal of Manufacturing Technology Management, 21 (8), 990-1012

Liu, G., Deitz, G, D. (2011), Linking supply chain management with mass customization capability. International Journal of Phys Distrb Logist Manag, 41 (7), 668-683.

Macaulay, J. (1996). Management in the agile organization (in Montgomery, J.C. and Levine, L.O. Eds), The Transition to Agile Manufacturing, ASQC Quality Press, Milwaukee, WI.

Maskell, B. H. (1991). Performance Measurement for World Class Manufacturing. Productivity Press, Portland, OR.

McBurney, D. H. (1994). Research methods, third edition. Pacific Grove, CA: Brooks/Cole Publishing.

McCarthy, I.P. (2004). Special issue editorial: the what, why and how of mass customization. Production, Planning & Control, 15, 347-351.

Medini,K.,Duigou, J,L., Cunha, C, D., Bernard, A (2015), Investigating mass customization and sustainability compatibilities, International Journal of Engineering, Science and Technology, 7 (1).

Meredith, S., Francis, D. (2000). Journey towards agility: the agile wheel explored, The TQM Magazine, 12 (2), 137 – 143.

Miles, M. B., and Huberman, A. M. (1994). Qualitative Data Analysis: A Sourcebook of New Methods, 2nd Ed, Thousand Oaks, CA: Sage.

Mostyn, B. (1995). The content analysis of qualitative research data: A dynamic approach. In M. Brenner, J. Brown and D. Canter (eds), The research interview: uses and approaches. London: Academic Press. Page 63

Narver, J. C., and Slater, S. F. (1990). The effect od a market orientation on business profitability. Journal of Marketing, 54 (4), 20-35.

Patton, M. Q. (1990). Qualitative Evaluation and Research Methods. Newbury Park, CA: Sage.

Pero, M., Abdelkafi, N., Slanesi., Blecler, T. (2010). A framework for the alignment of new product development and supply chain. International Journal of supply chain management, 15 (2), 115-128.

Piller, F.T. (2001). The myths of mass customization. Proceedings of the World Congress on Mass Customization and Personalization, Hong Kong University of Science and Technology, Hong Kong (October, 2001).

Piller F (2007) Observations on The Present and Future of Mass Customization. International J of Flex Manufacturing Systems 19:630–636

Pine, B. J. (1993). Mass Customization: The New Frontier in Business Competition. Boston MA: Harvard Business School Press.

Pine, B. J. (1993). Mass customizing products and services. Planning Review, 21 (4), 6-14.

Pine, B.J., Peppers, D., and Rogers, M. (1995). Do you want to keep your customers forever?. Harvard Business Review, 73 (2), 103-14.

Pine, B. J., Victor, B., and Boynton, A. C. (1993). Making mass customization work. Harvard Business Review, 71 (5), 108-109.

Roethlisberger, F. J. (1977). Elusive Phenomena of Organizational Behavior. Journal of Management Education, 31 (30), 321-338.

Rungtusanatham, Salvador, F. (2008). From Mass Production to Mass Customization: Hindrance factors, structural inertia and transition hazards, Production and Operations Management, 17, 385-396.

Salvato, C., Rerup, C. (2011). Beyond collective entities; multilevel research on organizational routines and capabilities. Journal of Management, 37 (2), 468-490.

Sarkis, J. (2001). Benchmarking for agility. Benchmarking. An International Journal, 8 (2), 88-107.

Schein, E. (1985). Organizational Culture and Leadership: A Dynamic View, Jossey-Bass, San Francisco, CA.

Senge, P. (1990). The Fifth Discipline. New York, NY: Doubleday.

Sharp, J.M., Irani, Z., Desai, S. (1999). Working towards agile manufacturing in UK industry. International Journal of Production Economics. 62 (1), 155-169.

Sheather, G. and Hanna, D. (2000), "Towards an integrated supply network model", The Journal of Enterprise Research Management, Australasian Production and Inventory Control Society, 3 (3), 5-10.

Sohal, A. S. (1996). Developing a lean production organization: an Australian case study. International Journal of Operations & Production Management, 16 (2), 91-102.

Stalk, G. (1998). The time – The next source of competitive advantage. Harvard Business Review, Jul-Aug 1988, 14-51.

Strauss, A., and Corbin, J. (1990). Basics of Qualitative

Research: Grounded Theory Procedures and Techniques. London: Sage.

Su, J, C, P., Chang, Y., Fergusaon, M., Ho, J, C. (2010). The impact of delayed differentiation in make-to-order environments. International Journal of Production Research, 48 (19), 5809-5829.

Ohno, T. (1998). Toyota Production System Beyond Large Scale Production. Productivity Press, New York, NY.

Tang, Z., Chen, X., and Xiao, J. (2005b). Operational tactics and tenets of a new manufacturing paradigm 'instant customization. International Journal of Production Research, 43 (14), 2873-2894.

Tang, Z., Chen, X., and Xiao, J. (2010). Using the classic ground theory approach to understand consumer purchase decision in relation to the first customized products. Journal of Product and Brand Management, 19 (3), 181-197.

Tersine, R.J., Wacker, J.G. (2000). Customer Aligned Inventory Strategies: Agility Mamixs. International Jounal of Agile Management System, 2 (2), 114-120.

Thaler, R. (1980). Towards a Positive Theory of Consumer Choice. Journal of Economic Behavior and Organization, 1 (1).

Treacy, M., and Wiersema, F. (1993). Customer intimacy and other value disciplines. Harvard Business Review.

Tu, Q., Vonderembse, M.A. and Ragu-Nathan, T.S. (2001). The impact of time-based manufacturing practices on mass customization and value to customer, Journal of Operations Management, 19, 201-17.

Ulrich, K.T. (1995). The role of product architecture in the manufacturing firm, Research Policy, 24 (3), 419-40.

Varadarajan, P.R., Jayachandran, S., Gimeno, J. (1999). The Theory of Multimarket Competition: A synthesis and implications for market strategy, 63 (3), 49-66.

Victor, B., and Boynton, A. (1998). Invented here: Maximizing Your Organization's Internal Growth and Profitability. Boston, MA: Harvard Business School Press.

Vonodh, S., Sundararai, G., Devadasan, S, R., Kuttalingam, D., Rajanavagam, D. (2010). Amalgation of mass customization and agile manufacturing concepts; the theory and implementation study in an electronics switches manufacturing company. International Journal of Production Research, 48 (7), 2141-2164.

Venkatraman, V. (2011). Inspired Take Your Dream from Concept to Shelf. John Wiley & Sons, NJ.

Veal, A.J. (2005). Business Research Methods: A Managerial Approach, 2nd Edition, Pearson Education Australia.

Wang,Z,.Chen,L,.Zhao,X,.Zhou,W. (2014). Modularity in building mass customization capability: The mediating effects of customization knowledge utilization and business process improvement, Science Direct, 34 (11), 678-687.

Walton, R. E. (1986). From control to commitment in the workplace. Harvard Business Review, 63, 76-84.

Weick, K. E. (1979). The social psychology of organizing. 2nd Ed Reading, MA: Addison-Wesley.

Wickens, P. (1993). Lean production and beyond the system, its critics and the future, Human Resource Management Journal, 3 (4), 75-89.

Wilkins, A. and Dyer, W Jr. (1988). Toward culturally sensitive theories of cultural change, Academy of Management Review, 13, 522-33.

White, B. J. (1988). Accelerating quality improvement. Presentation to the conference board, Total quality performance conference, New York, NY.

White, G. P. (1996). A meta-analysis model of manufacturing capabilities, Journal of Operations Management, 14, 315–331.

Wind, J., and Rangaswamy, A. (2001). Mass customization: The next revolution in mass customization. Journal of Interactive Marketing, 15 (1), 13-32.

Womack, J. P., Jones, D. T., and Roos, D. (1991). The machine that changed the world: The story of lean production. New York, NY: Macmillan.

Yilmaz, C., & Ergun, E. (2008). Organizational culture and firm effectiveness: An examination of relative effects of culture traits and the balanced culture hypothesis in an emerging economy. Journal of World Business, 43, 290-306.

Yin, R. K. (1994). Case Study Research: Design and Methods. Beverly Hills, CA: Sage.

Yin, R. K. (1991). Applications of case study research. Washington, DC: Cosmo Corp. page 52

Yinan, Q., Tang,M,.Zhang,M (2014), Mass Customization in Flat Organization, Journal of Applied Research and Technology, 2014,12(2).

Zhang, Z. and Sharifi, H. (2000). A methodology for achieving agility in manufacturing organizations", International Journal of Operations and Production Management, 20 (4), 496-512.

Zipkin, P. (2001). The limits of mass customization. MIT Sloan Management Review, 42, 81-87.

www.ingramcontent.com/pod-product-compliance
Lightning Source LLC
Chambersburg PA
CBHW031055180526
45163CB00002BA/840